Combating Corruption

A Comparative Review of Selected Legal Aspects
of State Practice and Major International Initiatives

W. Paatii Ofosu-Amaah
Raj Soopramanien
Kishor Uprety

© 1999 The International Bank for Reconstruction
and Development/THE WORLD BANK
1818 H Street, N.W.
Washington, D.C. 20433

Library of Congress Cataloging-in-Publication Data

Ofosu-Amaah, W.
    Combating corruption : a comparative review of selected legal
  aspects of state practice and major international initiatives / W. Paatii
  Ofosu-Amaah, Raj Soopramanien, Kishor Uprety.
    p.   cm.
  Includes bibliographical references.
  ISBN 0-8213-4523-0
    1. Political corruption—Developing countries. 2. Bribery—
  Developing countries. I. Soopramanien, Raj, 1950– . II. Uprety, Kishor,
  1958– . III. Title.
   K5261.033   1999
   345'.02323—dc21

                                                     99-30183
                                                    CIP

Contents

Foreword

The negative effects that corruption has on the development prospects of developing countries is becoming better understood over time. Since the Annual Meetings of the World Bank and the International Monetary Fund in October 1996, when the President of the World Bank, James Wolfensohn, offered World Bank assistance to member countries to devise and implement appropriate anticorruption strategies, international attention to the effects of corruption on development has grown markedly. Indeed, a number of major international agreements have been signed since then and countries around the world, whether developed or developing, have taken specific actions within their territories to combat the negative effects of corruption. The importance of an effective legal and judicial framework in the context of the combat against corruption has also been recognized, and countries are seeking ways in which they can strengthen such frameworks to deal with this issue. A major part of this work involves a better understanding of the approaches, mechanisms, instruments, and other tools, including legally related ones, that may be used.

This study, written by my colleagues in the World Bank's Legal Department, is timely for its attempts to review and analyze various legal and quasi-legal approaches and mechanisms used around the world in this combat against corruption. It should add to the growing volume of literature in this relatively new area of work for the Bank, and assist officials and Bank staff alike in gaining broad knowledge of some of the selected legal aspects relative to this important issue.

Andres Rigo
Acting Vice-President and General Counsel

Abstract

Corruption is not just a fact of life, it is also a worldwide phenomenon. In recent years, it has reached unprecedented levels. As recent events have demonstrated, no country, no matter how rich or powerful, can claim to be totally immune from the ravages that corruption wreaks. Using examples from across the globe, from Europe to Africa, from North America to Asia, the study provides a comparative review of selected legal aspects of state practice and international initiatives undertaken to fight corruption.

Although recognizing that different countries have used different techniques to combat corruption, the study proceeds at the outset to make a distinction between preventive and curative instruments that countries have resorted to in this regard. Preventive instruments consist of upstream legal rules and norms of good behavior conducive to the establishment of a corruption-free environment; curative instruments, consisting of anti-corruption laws proper, seek essentially to provide appropriate remedies to sanction acts of corruption that have occurred. While preventive instruments operate ex ante, curative laws seek to deal with corruption on an ex post basis.

Part II of the study reviews the preventive instruments of corruption, which it further subdivides under two separate headings, according to whether they represent a direct or an indirect method of combating corruption. Financial management, campaign financing, and procurement laws are cited as the three prime examples of preventive instruments of corruption, based on positive law sources, which rely almost exclusively on the direct method of combating corruption. Examples of the more indirect method reviewed in the study are codes of conduct, affirmations of national commitment, and leadership codes, as well as many other provisions relating to declarations of assets and freedom of information and the media.

The curative instruments of corruption are discussed in Part III of the study, which deals, successively, with the process of investigation of corruption offenses and the judicial process. Using examples of best practices from several jurisdictions, the study reviews the contents of corruption legislation, including applicable sanctions and penalties, the evolving definition of money laundering, and last but not least, the special rules of evidence applied from time to time to challenge some of the myths associated with the universally recognized presumption of innocence and thus facilitate the process of investigation and prosecution of corruption charges. Part III concludes with a brief discussion of some elements to be taken into account in the definition of corruption.

Although the study highlights some of the bold measures that have been undertaken by countries—with varying degrees of success—to combat corruption, it also recognizes that at a national level, the anticorruption agenda is at best unfinished. Hence, the emphasis on the international aspects of the fight against corruption, which is the subject matter of Part IV.

Numerous initiatives have been undertaken by the international community to assist countries in their struggle to contain the spread of corruption. Many such global initiatives have been spearheaded by the United Nations. Regional organizations, including the Organization of American States, the Organization for Economic Cooperation and Development, the Council of Europe, and the Global Coalition for Africa, have also followed suit, preferring, however, to adopt their own individual conventions or declarations, as the case may be. The study reviews in turn each of these various international initiatives, highlighting the common themes and varying perspectives that come into play, as well as the parallels between national and international law in this regard.

The study concludes that legal initiatives alone cannot make a difference; they are mere tools in the fight against corruption. The most successful initiatives have been those that have been backed up by the necessary will to fight corruption, coupled with the required level of resources needed to engage in and sustain the fight. No amount of rhetoric, declarations, or even legislation can be a fitting substitute for adequate political will and a genuine determination to arrest the spread of corruption.

Acknowledgments

We extend our most sincere thanks to Mr. Louis Forget for reviewing the study and providing insights and valuable suggestions in terms of both its structure and content. Thanks are also due to Ms. Françoise Bentchikou and Mr. Robert Hunja for their comments on an earlier draft of this study. We also extend our sincere appreciation to Mr. Andres Rigo for providing comments, suggestions, and encouragement.

Last but not least, we have to acknowledge the strong support and assistance of Linda Thompson, Laura Lalime-Mowry, Vivien Richardson, and Helene Selesneff-Kipreos. Without their valuable contribution, much of the research on which this desk study is based would not have been possible. There are also many others who provided support and encouragement in this endeavor, but who would rather remain anonymous. We are grateful—as indeed we should be—to all of them.

Our huge debt of gratitude notwithstanding, the views expressed in this study are ours and ours alone. So are the errors, omissions, and misstatements to be found therein.

I
Introduction

"Corruption's not of modern date;
It hath been tried in ev'ry state"

John Gray
Fables, 1738

According to the Oxford English Dictionary, "corruption" can occur in many forms. It can affect the "physical" in terms of the destruction or spoiling of anything, especially by disintegration or by decomposition with its attendant unwholesomeness and loathsomeness; it can affect "morals" by the "perversion" or "destruction" of integrity in the discharge of public duties by bribery or favor or the use or existence of corrupt practices. "Corruption" in the second sense is a phenomenon found in all societies, whether developed or developing. Its detrimental and corrosive effects know no bounds, but in developing countries, practices recognized as corrupt have had a much more debilitating effect than in developed countries. In many such societies, corruption exacts heavy economic costs, distorts the operation of free markets, slows down economic development, and destroys the ability of institutions and bureaucracies to deliver the services that society may expect. Corruption also casts a negative influence on the efforts to deal with the incidence of poverty. It has been stated that corruption is the mechanism by which a nouveau riche class has been developed in many societies, particularly in the developing world.[1] The effect of corruption on the economic fortunes of developing countries and its effect on life in the developed countries have therefore been the subject of many learned writings and articles, especially in recent times.[2]

Although surveys have shown that industrialized countries rank among the least corrupt, no country, rich or poor, can claim to be wholly virtuous.[3] In Western Europe[4], as in Japan and the United States[5], an abundance of cases in the daily press demonstrates how vulnerable every society, no matter how developed, is to corruption. In terms of the perceived levels of corruption in countries, the only difference between rich and poor countries is a matter of degree (see table 1).

Table 1. Perceived Corruption Index

Country	Corruption Index	GNP/Capita ($) PPP	Country	Corruption Index	GNP/Capita ($) PPP
Denmark	9.94	21,230	Belgium	5.25	21,660
Finland	9.48	17,760	Czech Rep.	5.20	9,770
Sweden	9.35	18,540	Hungary	5.18	6,410
New Zealand	9.23	16,360	Poland	5.08	5,400
Canada	9.10	21,130	Italy	5.03	19,870
Netherlands	9.03	19,950	Malaysia	5.01	9,020
Norway	8.92	21,940	South Africa	4.95	5,030
Australia	8.86	18,940	Korea, Rep. of	4.29	11,450
Singapore	8.66	22,770	Uruguay	4.14	6,630
Luxembourg	8.61	37,930	Brazil	3.56	5,400
Switzerland	8.61	25,860	Romania	3.44	4,360
Ireland	8.28	15,680	Turkey	3.21	5,580
Germany	8.23	20,070	Thailand	3.06	7,540
United Kingdom	8.22	19,260	Philippines	3.05	2,850
Israel	7.97	16,490	China	2.88	2,920
United States	7.61	26.980	Argentina	2.81	8,310
Austria	7.61	21,250	Venezuela	2.77	7,900
Hong Kong (China)	7.28	22,950	India	2.75	1,400
Portugal	6.97	12,670	Indonesia	2.72	3,800
France	6.66	21,030	Mexico	2.66	6,400
Japan	6.57	22,110	Pakistan	2.53	2,230
Costa Rica	6.45	5,850	Russia	2.27	4,480
Chile	6.05	9,520	Colombia	2.23	6,130
Spain	5.90	14,520	Bolivia	2.05	2,540
Greece	5.35	11,710	Nigeria	1.76	1,220

Note: Corruption Perception Index, from 0 to −10, with highest figure indicating least corruption.

Source: Transparency International. World Bank. (Table reproduced from *Financial Times,* September 16, 1997, p. 15. [Wolfe, Martin. "Corruption in the Spotlight"])

The definition of "corruption" and "corrupt practices" varies from country to country.[6] The World Bank and other multilateral institutions have defined it as "the abuse of public office for private gain."[7] It involves the seeking or exacting of a promise or receipt of a gift or any other advantage by a public servant in consideration for the performance or omission of an act, in violation of the duties required of the office. It may also involve extortion of monies or theft by public servants of amounts due or payable to public coffers. Corruption may also be found in the political context, where donations are made to political parties and politicians so that, upon assumption of power, favorable decisions and actions may be taken for the benefit of the contributors.[8] In recent times, the crime of money laundering has been added to the growing list of actions classified as corrupt practices. Money laundering is included because it involves actions designed to obscure the source of monies being used in the economic system, most of such funds originating from illegal acts, involving not just drug trafficking but corruption and other offenses as well. Indeed, as will be seen in the analysis of selected practices, mechanisms, and laws and regulations to be found in many areas of the world, much has been done and continues to be done to limit its incidence both in countries (national level) and at the international level.

An essential element in any discussion of corruption is the legal and judicial framework within which corruption exists and how it can—and often does—contribute to its demise. As noted above, all legal systems of the world include laws and sometimes institutions whose objectives are to stem the increase in corrupt activities. It is unquestioned that law is crucial in the fight against corruption, and this has as its basis the fact that rules included in the laws define how individuals ought to interact with each other. Law also provides the framework for the settlement of disputes and for dealing with the infringement by individuals of acts that society has deemed to be illegal and not in its interests. Thus, any effort to analyze or reduce corruption must include a clear understanding of a country's legal and judicial system.

From a domestic point of view, there are two separate, but complementary, aspects of the fight against corruption. The first consists of a set of upstream rules and norms of good behavior (codes of conduct, manifestos, declarations) conducive to a corruption-free society (preventive approach). The second aspect consists of anticorruption laws proper (general or specific legislative enactments), whose purpose is to provide appropriate remedies, including criminal sanctions and penalties, procedural rules, and institutional mechanisms, as needed, to combat acts of corruption that have already occurred (curative approach). The first aspect deals with corruption ex ante; the second aspect deals with corruption ex post. Most countries have resorted to a combination of both these approaches.

In addition, since the 1970s, the international community has been concerned about the negative effects of corruption on national developmental programs and the world's economy. Since then, several binding and nonbinding instruments have been adopted to guide national actions, promote international cooperation, and build support for fighting corruption.

This study reviews and analyzes legal and quasi-legal approaches and mechanisms that have been devised to combat corruption in various countries around the world. These selected approaches and mechanisms will be described, analyzed, and evaluated with the aim of drawing lessons of experience that might guide officials and professionals interested in the fight against the cancer of corruption. Parts II and III deal with the preventive and the curative approaches, respectively. The international dimensions and initiatives of the fight against corruption are discussed in Part IV.

II
Initiatives Conducive to a Corruption-Free Environment —A Preventive Approach

Legal instruments used to combat corruption vary from one country to another. Countries opt for instruments that are most appropriate to their economic, cultural, and sociopolitical situation. Some fight corruption indirectly through general provisions and notions embedded in their constitutions, or even informal rules of conduct without the force of law; others seek to control it more directly, using positive law sources, to regulate areas of human activity prone to corrupt practices. Because corrupt practices occur in various situations and require a variety of responses, most countries seek to contain corruption by use of a combination of all these approaches. Ultimately, the choices vary according to the political will, the nature and gravity of the corrupt actions identified, and their influence on society.

The preventive approach seeks not so much to sanction acts of corruption as to pre-empt them altogether. Its fundamental purpose is to deter corrupt practices and ensure that private and official activities are carried out and exercised in a corruption-free environment. This approach relies partly on implicit or indirect techniques based on customs, traditions, or soft law, and partly on explicit techniques based on positive law, including procurement, campaign financing, and financial management rules.

Indirect Technique

The indirect techniques of combating corruption discussed in this study are those pertaining to national commitment, leadership codes, declaration of assets, codes of conduct, and the role of the media, respectively.

National Commitment

General. The degree of development of a country is the product of not just sound economic policies but also compliance by political leaders, public officials, and citizens with laws, rules, and regulations, as well as adherence to codes of conduct. A compliant citizenry is more likely to exist in countries where public officials are not only competent, but also impartial and nonpredatory, and also where transparency and accountability prevail. Where officials are corrupt, compliance is seldom the optimal strategy for citizens, because bribery and illegal activity yield higher rewards. Rampant corruption tends to undermine the legitimacy of state institutions and governments. When a public official pursues his own interest without regard to the interests attached to his public function, the balance of authority both among government entities and between the state and civil society is effectively damaged.[9] If the general population assumes that public officials are not bound by the restraints of their public functions, it will be less likely to obey the laws of the society.[10] In such a situation, it is important to reiterate the preeminence of the rule of law, and more directly the need to combat corruption at the highest level, because it is one of the root causes of destabilizing the rule of law.

Several countries have attempted to articulate their willingness to combat corruption through hierarchically important legal texts in the legal system. The Constitution of the Fourth Republic of Ghana (1992), for instance, provides boldly: "The State shall take steps to eradicate corrupt practices and the abuse of power."[11] This provision conveys a strong message by the constitution makers as to the commitment of the country to prevent and combat corruption.

Nepal is another country that has used its constitution as one of the means of indicating its abhorrence of corruption. The eradication of corruption is a commitment of the state embodied in the constitution and for this purpose, Nepal's constitution provides specifically for the establishment of a Commission for the Investigation of Abuse of Authority.[12] This Authority is vested with the power to conduct inquiries into and investigate improper conduct or corruption by persons holding any public office.[13] Considering the importance of this commission, its Chief Commissioner is appointed by the king on the recommendation of the Constitutional Council.[14]

In the same spirit, the 1995 Constitution of Uganda takes a comprehensive approach and devotes an article to *accountability*. It emphasizes that all public offices are held in trust for the people; all persons placed in positions of leadership and responsibility are, in their work, answerable to the people; and finally all lawful measures will be taken to expose, combat, and eradicate corruption and abuse or misuse of power by those holding political and other public offices.[15]

In Ukraine, corruption has long ceased to be the sole domain of law enforcement authorities: it has now become an issue of national significance. For the first time, the new President, Leonid Kuchma, on July 21, 1994, signed the "Decree on Urgent Measures of Enhancing Struggle

Against Corruption." Pursuant to this decree, the president ordered the Ukrainian Ministry of the Interior, the Security Service, the State Customs Committee, the State Committee for Protection of the State Borders, the National Guards, the government of the Republic of Crimea, local executive bodies, and the Prosecutors General to pursue systematically coordinated measures aimed at essentially enhancing the fight against banditism, corruption, and other gross crimes. [16]

Interestingly, examples of legal and constitutional instruments that posit a state-level national commitment to curbing corruption are not commonplace. They are limited in number, of recent origin, and essentially from the developing world. The constitutions of most developed countries do not have similar provisions. Instead, the control of corrupt practices is left to the promulgation of legislation in the context of the legislative framework. In such cases, a statement of national commitment hardly brings any added value. Moreover, the civil society in these countries—where democratic institutions have operated for a significantly long period of time—is well versed in the issue of corruption and proactive toward its eradication.

Conclusion. Developed countries have been relatively successful in their fight against corruption, even in the absence of specific organic law provisions. While some countries in the developing world have included provisions intended to state their resolve to combat corruption, this has not so far yielded significant results. Indeed, in countries where corruption is endemic and generalized and institutions to combat it are still in embryonic form—or totally defunct, postulating norms of *state honesty, state integrity, and state commitment* through the promulgation of important legal texts, such as constitutions, can make a valuable contribution toward eradicating corruption[17]. At the very least, it illustrates how the body politic feels about this moral and development-related issue.

Leadership Codes

In the effort to prevent or combat corruption, the role as well as commitment of national political leaders is crucial. It is important for the national political leaders to be willing to implement measures that require them to sacrifice their own personal interests and establish good governance. In other words, the top leadership should set the tone for a system of governance that is transparent and agree to abide by it.[18] Such measures, mostly transpiring from state policy, are also, in some countries, incorporated in the constitutional or legislative instruments.

If not clarified at the outset, the term "leadership code" may be misleading. Coined initially in the context of African countries, a leadership code normally includes a series of rules (embedded in the organic or general laws or informal canons without force of law) that are deemed to be useful for combating corruption in a country, to be followed by, or recommended for, senior officials and leaders. The focus of such codes is on the leadership and bureaucracy of the particular country.

State Practice. With the intention of minimizing self-dealing by political leaders (or senior officials) and addressing the issue of conflict of interest, some African countries, such as Tanzania and Uganda, have adopted legislation that requires such leaders or officials to report potential for conflict of interest in their duties.[19] The Constitution of the Fourth Republic of Ghana (1992) goes further and provides an interesting and comprehensive example of the commitment of the state, specifies the norms of behavior of public officials, and indicates a strong state interest in the prevention of corrupt practices.

Conclusion. Although not yet part of the universal positive law, provisions encouraging leaders to lead by example are justified in all countries. This should especially be the case in countries that, for a variety of sociopolitical reasons, have failed to develop a satisfactory legal framework and where corruption is rampant at high levels of government and society. In such countries and situations, one way to control the propensity for corruption is to systematically reduce the incentives and opportunities for public leaders and officials to engage in corrupt practices. Indeed, in many countries, scandals and scams that involve high offices, political leaders, and senior officials have shaken the public's confidence in the way governments have performed throughout decades. Hence, codes of conduct inculcating a leadership dimension to the control of corruption may help uplift the frustration of the public and rebuild confidence in the state in general, and the establishment in particular.

Declaration of Assets

Introduction. Another technique used in the prevention of corruption is to expose the gains (primarily financial) that an official has reaped from corruption and, in so doing, question the legitimacy of its source or sources. This indirect technique of attacking corruption at destination necessitates that states proscribe and sanction a public official whose assets have increased substantially and unreasonably during his tenure in office, and who cannot explain such increase in terms of his lawful earnings. For this to happen, it is important for the state (or the general public, in some cases) to be able to compare the real financial worth of senior government officials before and after they assume office. Such financial worth becomes a crucial comparator when examining whether alleged corruption has occurred during and after the tenure in office. The declaration makes it easier to detect such corruption.

State Practice. Several countries have attempted to prevent corruption by providing for this type of preassessment system through constitutional or other legal means.

The 1992 Ghana constitution, for instance, requires any person who holds a public office to submit to the Auditor-General a written declaration of all property or assets owned by, or liabilities owed by, him or her, whether directly or indirectly, before taking office, at the end of every four years, and at the end of his or her term of office.[20] Such declaration can, on demand, be produced in evidence before a court of competent jurisdiction, a commission of inquiry, or an investigator appointed by the Commissioner for Human Rights and Administrative Justice,[21] which is a constitutionally mandated position. Based on the comparisons undertaken, any property or assets acquired by a public officer after the initial declaration and that is not reasonably attributable to income, gift, loan, inheritance, or any other legitimate source is deemed to have been acquired in contravention of the constitution.[22] The 1995 Constitution of Uganda has also made it a constitutional obligation for senior public officials to declare their assets (property) when they assume office and periodically thereafter.[23] A committee to which such declarations are to be made has also been created. Similarly, the Turkish constitution requires declarations of assets to be made by persons entering public service and those serving in the legislative and executive organs of government. The frequency of such declarations is governed by specific legislation.[24]

In March 1998, the Parliament of Mozambique approved an ethics law[25] that attempts to specify norms of conduct applicable to politically appointed officials. This law requires all politically appointed officials to submit formal declarations of assets and commercial affiliations upon taking office and to periodically update them. It is interesting to note, however, that the law does not cover civil servants who are also involved in the management of public institutions and resources and who remain highly vulnerable to corrupt practices. Despite this shortcoming, the Ethics Law of Mozambique may have an appropriate salutary effect on the conduct of all public servants.

In 1978, the United States introduced the Ethics in Government Act[26]. The Act requires financial disclosure by high government officials in all three branches of the federal government, restricts contacts between former high-level executive branch employees and their former agencies, and establishes a government office to monitor compliance with the law. A provision of the Ethics in Government Act establishes a mechanism for appointing an independent counsel to investigate and prosecute wrongdoing by high government officials.[27]

In Mauritius, every member of the National Assembly and every cabinet minister is required to deposit with the Clerk of the National Assembly a declaration of assets and liabilities in relation to self, spouse, and minor children and grandchildren.[28] They are required to specify any property sold, transferred, or donated to them in any form or manner.[29] Similarly, Singapore requires public servants to declare their assets each year and to keep free from debt.[30]

Expressing accountability through a public declaration is not a novel idea. A number of countries require those who wield executive power and elected representatives of the people in general to make their assets and liabilities public. In the Philippines, since the "people power" revolution of 1986, a law has been promulgated that requires the president and the cabinet to declare their assets and liabilities in a register accessible to the public. A number of other Asian countries, including India and Nepal, have also instituted systems to carry out such preassessment, albeit not necessarily as a legal or constitutional requirement.

Evidence in many countries suggests that laws relating to the declaration of assets have been on the books but seldom been taken seriously.[31] For example, to ensure enforcement of the measures stipulated in the Ethics Law of Mozambique, in early March 1998, the Mozambican government submitted a bill entitled "High Authority Against Corruption" (pursuant to which the authority was to be vested with power to investigate and prosecute corruption cases, including cases related to the declaration of assets) but Parliament rejected it without any debate. Similarly, to ensure a smooth implementation of the code of conduct stipulated in its constitution, Nigeria envisaged a Code of Conduct Bureau as well as a tribunal, but the tribunal has never been made operational, although members of the bureau were appointed.[32] A 1996 move in India to exclude elected representatives from the purview of the Indian Prevention of Corruption Act (1988) also shows the gap between the political will to curb corruption and related implementation measures.[33] The lessons of experience tend to point to a situation where assets are declared but appropriate mechanisms are not put in place to enforce violations.

Conclusion. Although the requirement that public officials should declare their assets has been helpful on its own merits, in practice it has not significantly curbed the incidence of corruption in any country. Indeed, the examples indicate that very few countries have established mechanisms to check the accuracy of the information provided. Also in many countries, the family and kinship systems make it difficult to ensure the accuracy of the information. The corrupt will always find ways to conceal their illicit gains by transferring them to friends or relatives while actually retaining control of them; and many legal systems remain unequipped to cope with this situation or use such declarations as a basis for successful enforcement actions. Some national laws have attempted to provide, in relation to the offenses of bribery and unexplained excessive wealth, that, where there is reason to believe that any person was holding assets on behalf of a person accused of corruption or to have acquired assets as a gift from such accused person, those assets shall be presumed to have been in the control of the accused.[34] However, despite these provisions, experience around the world indicates that implementation of the requirement of assets declaration has been less than formidable. Known instances of senior government officials being taken to court on grounds of having made a false declaration of assets (even where rumors are strong and rampant) are uncommon. Similarly, not many top government officials have ever been removed from office on grounds that they were not able to explain the assets shown in their declarations. To make matters worse, a generally accepted methodology for verifying the information contained in the declaration of assets and liabilities does not exist.

Notwithstanding such shortcomings, it should be further stressed that a system of disclosure of assets can be a powerful deterrent in its own right. Backed by an increased level of dissemination of information regarding declaration of assets worldwide, and coupled with efficient implementation and enforcement mechanisms (including mechanisms to check the accuracy and monitor failures to report), it can contribute—albeit modestly—to a country's effort to reduce and prevent the incidence of corruption.

Codes of Conduct

General. Codes of conduct are standards of good behavior that are prescribed from time to time in relation to groups of individuals, organizations, or professional bodies. The substance of the codes varies according to the functions, purposes, and objectives of such groups, bodies, or organizations. Although codes of conduct are, generally speaking, more informal, and their application generally less rigid than laws, there are instances of codes of conduct established in the form of laws and subject, accordingly, to the full force of the law, including the application of civil and criminal penalties. More often, however, codes of conduct are expressed in the nature of informal, but binding, rules of conduct that rely partly on peer pressure but partly also on other forms of internal professional discipline and self-policing mechanisms. Although these codes of conduct are not primarily meant as devises against financial corruption, they certainly contribute to the promotion of transparency and accountability, and in so doing, contribute—however indirectly—to the control of corruption in society.

Public Officials. In many countries, codes of conduct have been prescribed for civil servants and elected officials to govern their professional behavior and their dealings with other parties. In some countries, attempts have been made, particularly in the case of political leaders and other senior officials, to accord enforceability to rules of conduct by embodying such rules in the constitutional or legal framework.

Many of the codes of conduct governing the behavior of elected representatives as well as public appointees are self-explanatory. When monetary compensation is limited, there is a tendency to sell privileges.[35] Thus, an effective technique to assist in the prevention of corrupt practices is to establish a clear-cut code of conduct for public officers. The practices in several countries are illustrative of this approach.

State Practice. In Australia, the "Guidelines on Official Conduct of Commonwealth Public Servants," as amended in 1987, covers relationships among politicians and between their staff and public servants, as well as the treatment of public and official information. The guidelines also cover their participation in public interest groups, financial and other private interests, and personal behavior.[36]

The 1992 Constitution of Ghana also includes a comprehensive code of conduct for public officers.[37] For instance, it states that " a public officer shall not put himself in a position where his personal interest conflicts or is likely to conflict with the performance of the functions of his office."[38] Further, "no person shall be appointed or act as the chairman of the governing body of a public corporation or authority while he holds a position in the service of that corporation or authority."[39] These provisions establish the notions of incompatibility of offices and of conflict of interest.

The ethical conduct for public servants in Japan is prescribed in the National Public Service Law of 1948, which places primary focus on public interest and confidentiality. Standards of ethical conduct cover such items as service to the people, oath of service, obeying laws, prohibition of conduct causing discredit to the public service, preserving secrecy, restriction of political activity, and exclusion from private enterprises.[40]

As noted above, in March 1998, the Parliament of Mozambique approved an ethics law aimed at codifying the conduct of some officials. It defines the rights and responsibilities of governing officials and discourages acceptance of gifts by public officials.[41]

Gift acceptance by public officials has also been considered as seriously unethical under the laws of the United States. The Congressional Ethics Code of the United States (1977) lays out detailed provisions establishing standards of conduct, and limiting income earned over and above congressional salaries, honoraria fees, and gifts.[42]

Singapore's Prevention of Corruption Act and Hong Kong's Prevention of Bribery Ordinance, which are intended mainly to reduce the incidence of corruption among public employees, are also noteworthy in this context. In Singapore, public servants are forbidden to receive gifts, in money or in kind, from persons other than friends or family. There are no limits on gifts and loans from relations. The Hong Kong law, though not as strict, is quite specific. On special occasions, public officials can accept gifts not exceeding $130 (HK$) from the public and $260 from friends. At other times, friends can give gifts of HK$52 and loans of HK$260. Loans from the public cannot exceed HK$130.

Similar, though less detailed but stringent, provisions are stipulated in the Law on Status of a People's Deputy of Ukraine. For instance, Article 4 provides that the status of a People's Deputy is incompatible with the occupation of any other business or service position, except teaching, research, and other creative work. A People's Deputy cannot receive gifts or awards from foreign governments or foreign and Ukrainian institutions, organizations, and enterprises irrespective of their form of ownership, except for teaching, research, and other creative work. In addition, a People's Deputy of Ukraine must abide by other demands and limitations established by the legislation on fighting corruption. Any Deputy who violates the provisions of this law by taking a position incompatible with the position of Deputy can have his mandate annulled.

The Russian Antimonopoly Law[43] also adopts a similar approach, prohibiting state and government officials from engaging in independent entrepreneurial activity; owning enterprises; voting in the general meeting of economic partnerships or societies, either independently or through a representative; and holding office in any administrative structure of an economic entity. Officials of federal executive bodies, executive bodies of Russian Federation (RF) subjects and local self-government agencies, for-profit or nonprofit organizations or their managers, and individuals, including individual entrepreneurs, bear civil, administrative, or criminal liability for violations of any of the provisions of the Antimonopoly Law.

The control of travel by executive officials is another noteworthy aspect of the Russian legal framework. RF Presidential Decree No. 981[44] prohibits officials and executives of central federal bodies of the executive branch and managers and officials of the administration of the president of the RF and the staff of the RF government from taking official trips abroad at the expense of enterprises, institutions, organizations, or individuals doing business with the state. According to the decree, these officials shall also not take personal trips at the expense of any of these same entities. This prohibition against official trips abroad does not apply if such travel takes place in accordance with RF international agreements, or on a mutual basis pursuant to an agreement between the RF and a foreign state. However, there are no penalties specified in Decree No. 981 for individuals who violate its provisions.

Other Elected Officials and Professional Groups. Among the array of professional codes of conduct, those that have attracted the most attention in the context of the current debate on corruption are the ones dealing with political leaders[45] and judges.

Code of conduct of ministers: Ministers in the executive branch of the government play an important role in ensuring that government policies are implemented in a transparent and accountable manner. However, in situations where a minister who is a member of the government is also a member of a political party, accountabilities are blurred, and there is scope for corrupt acts to occur. It is important for the minister, accordingly, to clearly distinguish between his or her actions as a minister and actions as a member of a political party.[46]

The U.K. model: The United Kingdom's Code of Conduct and Guidance on Procedures for Ministers attempts to establish certain norms to that effect.[47] The U.K. code establishes guiding principles essentially based on the principles of integrity, honesty, and impartiality in public functions. In this context, it spells out the rules of conduct governing the ministers' overseas travel[48], the rules of protocol that apply to their dealings with foreign governments, and the privileges they, their spouses, or their advisers enjoy.

The provisions of the U.K. code stress that the ministers are expected to behave according to the highest standards of constitutional and personal conduct in the performance of their duties.[49] The proper use of public funds is key to the code. For instance, with respect to official facilities financed out of public funds, it specifies that such facilities should be used only for publicizing and advertising the activities of government, but not for the dissemination of materials related to the minister's political party.

According to the U.K. Code, it is the duty of ministers to uphold the political impartiality of the Civil Service and not to ask civil servants to act in any way that would conflict with the Civil Service Code. It is their duty to ensure that influence over appointments is not abused for partisan purposes.[50] Similarly, the code makes it clear that ministers should ensure that no conflict arises, or appears to arise, between their private interests (financial or otherwise) and their public duties.[51]

Finally, the U.K. Code prohibits ministers from accepting a gift from anyone to whom the minister would then be obligated. Paragraph 126 of the Ministerial Code states: "It is a well-established and recognized rule that no minister or public servant should accept gifts, hospitality or services from anyone which would or might appear to place him or her under an obligation."[52]

Code of conduct of judges—the Madagascar example: Like ministers, judges are expected to behave according to the highest possible norms of propriety for justice to be credible. To deal with the credibility gap of judges in Madagascar, in 1997 a comprehensive code of conduct for judges was issued in the form of a *Circulaire* from the Minister of Justice.[53] Although primarily concerned with the rights and duties of judges, the Malagasy Code of Conduct of Judges also covers other officials who are directly or indirectly involved in the administration of justice. In essence, the relatively detailed code acknowledges that the standard of conduct of the judges and such officials should be above reproach and certainly higher than those being judged, and that their public personae should leave no grey area that could raise questions about their integrity and honesty.

The code prohibits judges from taking or accepting any monetary advantage from the treasury beyond what is provisioned in the laws governing their terms of service. The judges should refrain from taking any unlawful perquisites by interpreting them as a necessity or an inevitable precondition for the performance of their duties. According to the code, the judges must disengage themselves from any direct or indirect involvement in any business or profession and in any sale or purchase of or any dealings in shares, debentures, or any other similar financial instruments, and they must abstain from hearing any case involving a corporate or business entity in which they or their immediate relatives have interests. They are expected to decline any donations or gifts from any organizations or persons who could undermine or influence their performance as judges. In addition, they are to strictly refrain from any fund-raising activities. In short, judges are required to maintain the highest honor and dignity of their high offices.

Code of conduct of judges—the American model: There are many similarities but also striking differences between the Malagasy code and the code of conduct applicable to federal judges in the United States. The United States Code deals in an elaborate fashion with, among other things, the methodology of compensation of judges, an important vehicle for controlling corruption in courts.[54] The code provides that a judge may receive compensation and reimbursement of expenses for the law-related and extrajudicial activities permitted by the code, *if the source of such payments does not give the appearance of influencing the judge in the judge's judicial duties or otherwise give the appearance of impropriety* [emphasis added][55]. In addition, for purposes of clarity, the code specifies that compensation should not exceed a reasonable amount, nor should it exceed what a person who is not a judge would receive for the same activity. According to the code, reimbursement for expenses should be limited to the actual costs of travel, food, and lodging reasonably incurred by the judge and, where appropriate to the occasion, by the judge's spouse or relative. Any payment in excess of such an amount is considered to be compensation. Finally, the code requires a judge to make financial disclosures in compliance with applicable statutes and Judicial Conference regulations and directives.[56]

In the United States, additional restrictions on the receipt of compensation by judges are imposed by the Ethics Reform Act of 1989 and regulations promulgated by the Judicial Conference thereunder. The restrictions include, but are not limited to (a) a prohibition against receiving "honoraria" (defined as anything of value received for a speech, appearance, or article); (b) a prohibition against receiving compensation for service as a director, trustee, or officer of a profit or nonprofit organization; (c) a requirement that compensated teaching activities receive prior approval; and (d) a 15 percent limitation on the receipt of "outside earned income."[57]

Conclusion. Codes of conduct have at least two distinct advantages. First, even in the absence of enforceability, and even where a particular form of behavior falls short of a criminal offense, the existence of the code can still provide appropriate disincentives for corrupt activities. An improper act of a professional nature can be questioned by peers, and the professional group may take actions according to the mores of the group. Second, codes of conduct can serve as the catalyst for criminal proceedings.

Whether such codes originate in an organic law, a parliamentary enactment, or a mere informal code of behavior, there is growing recognition that a consistent set of rules of behavior, which promotes transparency and condemns abuse or misuse of power, is a powerful tool for the prevention of corruption within any group of officials, organization, or professional body.

Proactive Media

There is clearly a direct link between corruption in the public service and the lack of accountability on the part of public servants. One way to make public servants more accountable is to promote efficient and proactive mass media. The media (the Fourth Estate) play a key role in investigating allegations of impropriety in public affairs and exposing corruption and corrupt practices[58]. This role pertaining to denunciation of corruption becomes even more important when existing political institutions are inadequate and inefficient in ensuring accountability of public servants. Every governmental entity needs to be subjected to scrutiny, either directly, through the public eye, or indirectly, through the mass media.[59]

Role of the Media in the Context of Freedom of Expression. The mass media as the main expression of public opinion have long been recognized as having a role to play in ensuring that governments are accountable to the governed. Credible media exercise strong influence over the public and play an important part in revealing improper and unfair administrative actions and corruption. A good illustration of this is the role the media played in the Lockheed scandal, which prompted the resignation of the then-Prime Minister of Japan after allegations were made by a local monthly magazine.[60] Other examples abound.

In the last few decades, political liberalization in many countries has gradually made the media more powerful. Because of their efforts in gathering information, governments are becoming more accountable to their people or at least ensuring a modicum of transparency with respect to governmental action. Indeed, the media in some countries have demonstrated tenacity and unearthed information that law enforcement officials would not have been able to obtain, thereby making the media a prime source of potentially useful information, including information regarding acts of corruption committed in the society. Therefore, the media are, in the present-day world, not only passive spectators of the affairs of government but also active participants with increasing responsibility in society.

To enable the media to play their role, that of "divulger" of governmental action—including corrupt practices, a necessary precondition has been the grant of legally sanctioned protections. The media need a guarantee of unrestricted discussion of public affairs, among other things, through freedom of expression or inviolability of privileged information, and they should be given the possibility to organize, as well as the autonomy to act and react, as an institution. Journalists should, however, not be compelled to reveal their sources. Only a few countries worldwide have laws that provide such guarantees, and, even in such cases, these protections are not absolute.

The most important protection for the media is the guarantee of freedom of expression. In theory, this guarantee has already become commonplace in most constitutions and is often encompassed under the fundamental rights chapter of most constitutions. But, often again, such provisions are not always implemented. Only a few countries, such as the United States, are dedicated to making this fundamental human right a reality in practice. The First Amendment of the U.S. Constitution decrees that "Congress shall make no law . . . abridging the freedom of speech, or of the press . . . ." This constitutional provision for freedom of expression has been interpreted in a variety of ways in the courts and academic publications. The interpretations range from those that take a near-absolutist view that "no law" really means *no law* (a literal interpretation), to those that defend the theory of preferred position (of individuals), to those that take the approach of balancing interests, to those that advocate limited rights.[61] In spite of the noticeable contrast in the different views, the usefulness of the media is now undeniably established. Indeed, responsible and forthright media interested in presenting facts to the general public have thus become a *sine qua non* for a society that aims at preventing corruption.

Consistent with the principles underlying the U.S. constitutional provisions, many countries—either through their respective constitutions or specific legislation—have accorded an important role to the notion of the independence of the media. The Constitution of the Fourth Republic of Ghana, for instance, devotes a chapter to the freedom and independence of the media[62] and provides for a National Media Commission to administer press freedom and also to develop principles under which the press will operate.[63] A similar provision is to be found in the Constitution of Nigeria, which states that "the press, radio, television and other agencies of the mass media shall at all times be free to uphold the fundamental objectives [of the constitution] and uphold the responsibility and accountability of the government to the people."[64]

Not all constitutions devote a separate chapter to covering the role of the media. In India, for instance, freedom of the press is part of the freedom of speech and expression guaranteed by Article 19(1)(a) of the constitution. There is no specific provision ensuring freedom of the press. Freedom of the press is regarded as a "species" of which freedom of expression is the "genus."[65] Thus, as only a right flowing from the fundamental right of freedom of speech, freedom of the press in India stands on no higher footing than the freedom of speech of a citizen.[66] The effect, however, is to give the press the same rights as may be found in those countries that have emphasized the importance of the press through a separate provision in their constitutions.

Even though the importance of the media has been recognized by almost all the principal legal systems, and the principle of freedom of the media has become part of the organic laws in many countries, nonetheless there is still a significant gap between practice and theory. Indeed, in spite of similarity of constitutional provisions, the performance of the media in, for instance, Nigeria or Pakistan cannot be compared with that in the United States or France. The role of the media in providing ammunition for the fight against corruption is vital. Accordingly, it is necessary not just to provide the media with the freedom required for them to play this role but also to ensure that this freedom is not subject to unwarranted limitations in terms of cumbersome individual legal rights (libel), infringement of journalists' pledge of confidentiality, or compelling necessities of the states (secrecy).

Role of the Media in the Context of Libel Laws. In spite of the freedom of the media granted by constitutions, journalists (and media in general) continue to face a serious legal problem: the danger of being sued for libel or slander. The fear of libel suits, as a consequence, often leads journalists to suppress stories they would otherwise publish. The threat of suits, however, helps to bring discipline to the media in that they have to be responsible and develop methods to ensure that their publications reflect the facts.

The mere right to sue for libel gives people with real or imagined grievances an unparalleled opportunity to harass the mass media, regardless of whether they actually have a valid complaint. In the United States, for instance, a person suing for libel has the right to ask questions on a wide variety of issues during the pretrial discovery process. Those who have received unfavorable publicity sometimes may sue for libel merely as a means of identifying a whistleblower who helped a reporter gather information. Because the refusal to name a news source may be deemed an admission that no source exists, the media face the perennial dilemma of whether to reveal the identity of the confidential sources, to defend themselves against costly libel suits, or not to reveal the source and lose the suit.

Journalists' Pledge of Confidentiality. Journalists are often given inside information that no law enforcement officer could hope to obtain. Investigative journalists unearth confidential information of importance and often publish it without revealing their sources, as they are bound to by their rules of ethics or by the confidential nature of the sources. Without confidential sources, journalists would not be able to report many important news stories. It is common for whistleblowers (people with inside information about wrongdoing in government) to come forward and talk to a reporter in secret, something they would not do without a pledge of confidentiality.[67] Journalists thus are ethically obliged to protect the confidentiality of news sources. This pledge of confidentiality is a privilege of journalists that is widely recognized. However, in the interests of fairness and justice, judges in all jurisdictions would like all relevant information to be made available in court, and they are increasingly using their contempt of court power to enforce orders requiring journalists to supply confidential information.

In this context, it should be noted that the journalists' privilege (to maintain confidentiality of sources) is largely a 20th century idea developed in the United States. In 1896, the state of Maryland adopted a statutory shield law shielding a reporter from the duty to reveal sources of information.[68] In 1933, the state of New Jersey, and successively many other states, followed suit. More than half of the states in the United States now have such shield laws.[69] Because of widely varying judicial interpretations provided by different jurisdictions, it is difficult to generalize about the effectiveness of the state shield laws. Notwithstanding the absence of shield laws, the First Amendment of the U.S. Constitution (which provides for freedom of speech and of the press) protects the rights of journalists to keep their sources confidential, at least in the United States.

Role of the Media in the Context of Secrecy Rule. Another important dimension of the principle of freedom of information is how one would limit this role of the media in the light of a compelling high interest—that is, the need for a degree of secrecy on the part of government to assure the effectiveness of its operations. The role of the media is inevitably subject to the perennial conflict between the government's need for secrecy in certain areas to protect the public interest, and the public's need for free access to information to ensure that all public policy issues are discussed. The ability of the citizens to control governments is an inherent feature of any democracy. However, the present balance in a large majority of countries is tilted toward secrecy on the part of administrative agencies.

Only a few countries have accorded their citizens the right and access to a significant amount of government-related information. The four Scandinavian countries, the United States, Canada, and Hungary have a long history of public access to information.[70] In Sweden, for instance, the principle of access to information was established as early as 1766 as part of the Freedom of the Press Act.[71] In the United States, besides the protection granted by the constitution, the Administrative Procedures Act of 1946 requires the routine disclosure of government-held information. The most important piece of legislation, however, is the Freedom of Information Act of 1966 (FOIA), which replaced the provisions of the 1946 Act and states unequivocally that public access to most documents is to be the general rule. Most significantly, it listed the types of documents that could be kept secret (in nine general categories of exemption) and included provisions for the challenge by any citizen of a decision to withhold information.[72] Under the FOIA, virtually every record possessed by a federal agency must be made available to the public in one form or another unless it is specifically exempted from disclosure or specially excluded from the coverage of the Act in the first place.[73] The nine exemptions of the FOIA ordinarily provide the only bases for nondisclosure, and they are generally discretionary, not mandatory, in nature.

The Ugandan Constitution provides its citizens with the right of access to information. According to that constitution, every citizen has a right of access to information in the possession of the state or any other organ or agency of the state, except where the release of the information is likely to prejudice the security or sovereignty of the state or interfere with the right to privacy of any other person.[74] In Nepal, the right to information is a constitutional right.[75] In spite of the legal or constitutional provisions, however, citizens in countries such as Uganda or Nepal have not taken advantage of the right to information to the same extent as the citizens in developed countries.

In contrast, in most countries where the right to free access to information is not yet established, the decision to withhold administrative information or refuse access to documents is at the discretion of the executive branch of government. Such governments are free to withhold any information not only for legitimate reasons, such as the protection of national security or personal privacy, but also to protect themselves from criticism of wrongdoing, embarrassment, or inconvenience. This state of affairs is not conducive to good government and directly or indirectly fosters corruption.

Conclusion. The media's influence on building public opinion has, in many countries around the globe, been one of the indirect, but helpful, tools in the reduction of corrupt acts and practices in government. The media can also be used to emphasize and publicize the positive side of the country's efforts to prevent corruption. Indeed, it may be more than just a matter of coincidence that—with the exception of some countries such as India where the press enjoys near-absolute freedom, or Singapore, where the incidence of corruption is remarkably low—corruption appears to be most rampant in countries without a free, active, and objective press. Thus, there appears to be some correlation in the depth of corruption between those countries where the press enjoys significant freedoms and those where its rights are circumscribed.

Direct Technique

Campaign finance and procurement have been cited as two of the major sources of corruption, as has the absence of adequate financial management rules. Not surprisingly, therefore, much of the debate on corruption has focused on the contents of financial management, procurement, and campaign finance laws and their application. Along with financial management laws, procurement and campaign finance laws are regularly cited as some of the positive law sources that have a significant role to play in the campaign against corruption.

Transparent Financial Management System

Purpose. In a broad sense, the public sector financial management system encompasses the process of budget preparation, internal controls, and accounting. The financial management practices of most countries vary according to the nature of their political system. It may be centralized or decentralized, federated or unitary. Whatever the form, a general review of practices reveals that, in countries seeking to establish and maintain sound financial management systems, a distinction is imposed, often by law, among (a) the public entity that requests that an expenditure be made; (b) the budget division of the ministry of finance, which accepts the expense and gives the order to pay; and (c) the treasury, which actually makes payment. Systematically, these three distinct levels of acts are carried out by separate entities. To ensure smooth implementation of the process, emphasis is laid on a legal framework that governs transparent planning processes and internal check-and-balance mechanisms, as well as ex post supervisory role by an apex body. In short, a public accounting system capable of reporting on all expenditures has been considered indispensable for a country's good governance.

Financial Management. An appropriate legal framework is required to allow government agents to implement the budget, trace the financial records and statements, and control the implementation and accounting of expenses. This may take the form of constitutional provisions, laws and regulations, or both. Examples of such laws and regulations are the finance law itself, the laws on the organizational structures mandated to deal with the execution and control of state budgets, the budget law, and rules regarding bookkeeping for funds and property. Legal instruments vary from one country to the other.[76]

Budget execution law ensures that expenditures are consistent with the limits set out in the annual budget law (or laws) and with the requirements of other financial legislation and regulations. From a legal standpoint, budget execution is thus the practical application of the spending authority granted by the budget law. Accounting and auditing, though often considered as separate operations, are regarded as the final stage of budget execution. There is no phase of financial activity that is not controlled and directed, in some manner or other, by law.[77]

A comprehensive example of a legal framework for financial reporting is provided by the United States. In accordance with Section 3515 of the U.S. Federal Financial Management Act,[78] not later than March 1 in each year, the head of each executive agency is required to prepare and submit to the Director of the Office of Management and Budget[79] an audited financial statement for the preceding fiscal year, covering all accounts and associated activities of each office, bureau, and activity of the agency.[80] Each such audited financial statement of an executive agency shall reflect the overall financial position of the offices, bureaus, and activities covered by the statement, including assets and liabilities thereof; and results of operations of those offices, bureaus, and activities. The Director of the Office of Management and Budget prescribes the form and content of the financial statements of executive agencies, consistent with applicable accounting and financial reporting principles, standards, and requirements.[81]

One important precondition of transparency in financial management is the establishment of a mechanism for checks and balances. An adequate and effective financial management system presupposes that there is in place a mechanism permitting overall direction and control of the countries' finances. In the case of the United States, for instance, the Comptroller General is vested with the authority to prescribe accounting requirements, systems, and information. Section 3511(a) the Financial Management Act states:

> The Comptroller General shall prescribe the accounting principles, standards, and requirements that the head of each executive agency shall observe. Before prescribing the principles,

standards, and requirements, the Comptroller General shall consult with the Secretary of the Treasury and the President on their accounting, financial reporting, and budgetary needs, and shall consider the needs of the heads of the other executive agencies.

As the U.S. example illustrates, an effective internal control system, and one that promotes accountability, presupposes that all government entities must apply uniform accounting rules, principles, and standards.

In every sound financial management process, there is the need for submission of the entire financial statements to an apex body for ex post supervision. The U.S. law requires that, not later than March 31 of each year, the Secretary of the Treasury, in coordination with the Director of the Office of Management and Budget, prepare and submit to the President and the Congress an audited financial statement for the preceding fiscal year, covering all accounts and associated activities of the executive branch of the U.S. government. The financial statement reflects the overall financial position, including assets and liabilities, and results of operations of the executive branch of the U.S. government, and is prepared in accordance with the form and content requirements set forth by the Director of the Office of Management and Budget.[82] The Comptroller General of the United States audits this financial statement.[83]

Public Accounts Committees. Many countries, particularly those with a common-law tradition, have parliamentary committees responsible for monitoring public accounts that are known as Public Accounts Committees (PACs). PACs ensure ex post supervision of the financial management process. Mostly stemming from the states' constitutional provisions, these committees have the responsibility of ensuring ex post that all public funds are spent for purposes for which they are released. The members of these committees are often parliamentarians from different political parties. Parliamentary practice often requires that these committees be chaired by leaders of the opposition parties in the parliament. This practice provides an additional dimension of the financial checks and balances system, an essential element of a corruption-free society. However, it also carries the potential risk of unduly politicizing debates and neglecting its purely technical and financial aspects. Nonetheless, the existence of PACs assists in promoting a culture of accountability on the part of public officials.

Office of the Auditor General. In the process of financial management of a country, the role of the Office of the Auditor General (OAG) is also noteworthy. In many countries, the OAG or its equivalent is the organ of a state that has the responsibility of conducting independent audits and examinations that provide objective information, advice, and assurance to the parliament. Given the importance of the role the OAG fulfills, in most countries, the Auditor General is an independent officer appointed by the head of state or the parliament under an organic law.

In a general context, the Auditor General's responsibility is to audit and report to the parliament on the financial management and administrative practices of government agencies in order to enhance public sector accountability and performance. In a broader context, the Auditor General serves the public interest. The Auditor General, in his or her role as the principal provider to the parliament of independent and impartial information on public sector accountability and performance, serves as a "watchdog," guarding against waste of taxpayers' resources and checking that government delivers services in an equitable, efficient, and effective manner for the benefit of the citizens as a whole.

The Auditor General is thus an ally of the people and the parliament. He must act, and be seen to be acting, independently in carrying out all of his or her powers and duties. This independence is the cornerstone of public sector audit; and, therefore, to properly discharge his responsibilities, the Auditor General must be free from pressure, influence, or interference from any source that may erode that independence, another important element in the fight against corruption.

As in the case of the Office of the Comptrollers General, Auditors General are generally treated as constitutional entities. The appointment and dismissal of the heads of such institutions are often made pursuant to constitutional provisions.[84] In the absence of such constitutional provisions, many states use organic laws. In most countries, these entities report directly to the parliament and the head of state. Direct accountability of these entities to the parliament safeguards their independence and ensures that they are not subservient to political leaders.

Specific Features of Countries with Civil Law Traditions. In countries with legal systems deriving from civil law traditions, the practice of financial management and related principles is not much different. Among countries that have an appropriate financial reporting, accounting, and auditing system, one can observe a common legal and institutional framework. A set of financial accounting and auditing laws is generally found to be in place. Budget laws provide for responsibilities of government in the area of public accounting. Also, laws impose clear classification systems permitting the allocation of resources to the different functions of government and the use of such resources.

In addition, many countries have established administrative tribunals (*tribunais de contas*, in lusophone countries, or *cours des comptes* in francophone countries), completely autonomous institutions to deal with matters of public accounts. In France, for instance, there are courts charged with dealing with these matters. Such courts have both judicial and nonjudicial functions. They operate at both the national and regional levels. In the exercise of their judicial functions at a regional level, they sit as *chambres régionales des comptes* and examine and approve all public expenditures of the state departments and municipalities. In parallel, they exercise administrative supervision of public funds at the same regional level and can make reports that contribute significantly to an understanding of patterns of use of public funds. Against judgments of these *chambres régionales des comptes*, an appeal lies to the national *cour des comptes*. At the central level, the *Cour des comptes* is primarily responsible for auditing the accounts of state treasuries and paymasters and for supervising the carrying out by the appropriate officials of budgetary measures decided by the National Assembly. These accounting functions are coupled with judicial powers in that the *cour des comptes* can order rectification of errors made by the officials it supervises and, in appropriate cases, impose sanctions. In addition to the *cour des comptes*, there also exists in France the *cour de discipline budgétaire et financière*, which can deal with any irregularities committed by public officials responsible for implementing state and local authority budgets.[85]

Conclusion. Without adequate accounting, auditing, and financial reporting systems, it is impossible for a country to monitor expenditures and integrity of accounts. In the absence of such systems, misallocation or misappropriation of funds can easily occur and corruption can go undetected. Hence, whether regulated by law or not, it is imperative for countries to find and maintain systems that permit them to keep track of the sources, use, and the destination of public funds. This is the most important aspect of financial management for a society that seeks to be corruption-free.

Campaign Financing

Campaign financing is a major source of corruption in any modern democratic society. Many of the major scandals that have rocked democracies during the past decade have been linked in one way or another to campaign financing. If unchecked, it has the potential to discredit the society and pervert the democratic process. No review of anticorruption legislation is therefore complete without a careful analysis of campaign finance legislation.

The many cash-for-favors scandals associated with campaign financing are not peculiar to democracies. Tyrants, dictators, military leaders, and other self-appointed rulers alike rely on a coterie of loyal supporters and sycophants to consolidate their hold on power and compensate for the lack of legitimacy of their regimes. Even though campaign finance restrictions as such may never have been uppermost in the minds of such illegitimate leaders, the system of payoffs and kickbacks that they need to ensure their political survival is strongly reminiscent of the cash-for-favors scandals that have plagued the election process in modern democracies during the past decade.

In the United Kingdom, according to newspaper reports, one in three of the ruling Labor Party's biggest donors in the last general election has gained a peerage, a ministerial position, or an advisory role on policy after giving millions of pounds sterling to finance the party's election war chest[86]. In France, a former prime minister was being investigated for allegedly approving the creation of 26 fictitious positions in the city government of Paris. It was alleged that the creation of the so-called "ghost" positions amounted to a breach of recently adopted French campaign finance legislation. In the United States, there was speculation that the Attorney General would yield to growing demands for an independent counsel to investigate alleged illegal campaign contributions and other breaches of campaign finance legislation. Three sets of scandals that have dominated the headlines in three major democracies illustrate the growing impact of campaign financing on democratic society and its potential to unravel anticorruption efforts in established and emerging democracies alike.

Scope and Purpose of Campaign Finance Regulation. Campaign finance regulation varies from one country to another. Theoretically, there are at least three main purposes that it can serve. First, it serves to set overall spending limits. Second, it serves to set limits on campaign contributions, including limits on individual campaign contributions. Finally, it establishes disclosure rules and promotes transparency. Typically, there are also rules governing contributions by foreign nationals, as well as detailed rules governing record-keeping and the role, during elections, of the election supervision commission.

The purpose of spending limits is to keep to a minimum the pernicious effect of money both on politics and on the decisionmaking process. Limits on individual campaign contributions serve to reduce the potential influence of individual contributors and, in so doing, preserve the integrity of the political process. The combined effect of the spending limits and campaign contribution limits is to prevent the rich from exerting a disproportionate influence on politics, thus ensuring that the principle of political equality is maintained and adhered to.[87]

The United Kingdom. Campaign finance in the United Kingdom is governed by the Representation of the People Act (1983). The Act has provisions to control and limit candidates' overall election expenses, but not campaign contributions. Accordingly, the disclosure provisions of the Act are limited to candidates' election expenses. There are no restrictions on campaign contributions other than those resulting from the prescribed overall spending limits and, accordingly, no obligation to disclose the source or origin of campaign contributions.

The Act prescribes overall spending limits based on the number of registered voters, and according to whether the election is a parliamentary or local government election.[88] It provides, among other things, that no expenses aimed at promoting candidates, or securing their election or the defeat of another candidate, shall be incurred otherwise than by the candidates themselves or on their behalf.[89] Where any person other than the candidate or an agent acting on the candidate's behalf incurs expenses on behalf of a candidate, that person is required under the Act to submit a report to that effect to the relevant authorities, giving full particulars of the amount of the expenses and their purposes.[90]

At the end of the election cycle, all candidates are required to submit to the appropriate authorities a return, along with a declaration, giving details of the overall expenses incurred on their behalf for purposes of the election, as well as full particulars of the candidate's personal expenses, paid and unpaid claims, and disputed claims, if any.[91] Returns and declarations submitted by candidates or on their behalf are kept by the appropriate authorities and made available for inspection.[92]

Mauritius. In Mauritius, the Representation of the People Act 1958 is based on an earlier version of the U.K. Representation of the People Act. Like its U.K. counterpart, this Act makes no attempt to control or restrict campaign contributions. Accordingly, the provisions governing election expenses are solely concerned with overall spending restrictions,[93] as are the disclosure provisions.[94] As in the case of the United Kingdom, the Act provides that no expenditure in respect of a candidate shall be incurred otherwise than by the candidate himself or on his behalf.[95]

Where any person incurs expenditures in respect of a candidate in excess of the authorized amount, or without proper authority, both that person and the candidate in respect of whom the expenditures are incurred are deemed to be guilty of an illegal practice under the Act.[96] In the case of candidates, however, it is expressly provided that they shall not be guilty of an illegal practice unless it is proved that the expenditure was incurred with their consent.[97]

General Observations. Both the U.K. Representation of the People Act 1983 and the Mauritius Representation of the People Act 1958 are based on the somewhat simplistic assumption that all election expenses incurred in respect of a candidate will be authorized by the candidate or an agent acting on his behalf. There is no provision in either Act governing so-called independent expenditures, or expenditures expressly advocating the election or the defeat of a clearly identified candidate but made without prearrangement or coordination with a candidate, or party expenditures. Nor is there any reference in either of the Acts to the treatment of issue advocacy, a device made famous in the last U.S. presidential elections by a well-orchestrated blitz of issue advertisements designed, according to critics, not so much to promote specific issues, as their name implies, but to actually promote candidates. In so doing, both Acts blissfully avoid some of the complex campaign finance issues that have plagued U.S. elections in recent years.

In the case of Mauritius, although there is no specific reference to independent expenditures as such, there is nonetheless a clear recognition that candidates cannot be held criminally accountable for expenditures incurred on their behalf, but without their consent, by a third party.[98] Notwithstanding the provision that no expenditure in respect of candidates shall be incurred otherwise than by the candidates themselves or on their behalf,[99] it is arguable that candidates cannot be held financially accountable, either, for such expenditures incurred by a third party on his own initiative, and that such expenditures cannot count against a candidate's total spending limits.

The United States. Federal elections campaign finance in the United States is governed by the Federal Election Campaign Act (FECA).[100] Unlike the U.K. model, FECA focuses not just on spending limits, but on campaign contributions and related disclosure requirements as well. The courts in the United States have consistently upheld the right of Congress to regulate campaign contributions and impose strict disclosure requirements, affirming time and again that the primary purpose of FECA is to regulate campaign contributions and expenditures in order to eliminate the pernicious influence, actual or perceived, over candidates by those who contribute large sums.[101] Rejecting suggestions that the effect of FECA was to limit the right of free speech or freedom of association, the courts have stressed that the primary government interest recognized with respect to FECA's contribution limits is the interest in preventing corruption or the appearance thereof in the political process.[102]

FECA establishes a series of restrictions and limitations on campaign contributions and expenditures, including dollar limits on federal election campaign expenditures and, in the case of contributions, a ceiling of $1,000 on individual contributions to any candidate with respect to any election for federal office,[103] and another ceiling of $25,000 on the aggregate contributions of any individual in any calendar year.[104] Other restrictions apply to contributions made by or for the benefit of political committees.[105] Unlike the U.K. legislation,[106] FECA also goes on to impose an absolute ban on contributions by foreign nationals.[107]

The central feature of FECA, however, is its elaborate disclosure provisions. As the U.S. Supreme Court has pointed out in one famous case,[108] disclosure requirements deter actual corruption and avoid the appearance of corruption by exposing large contributions and expenditures to the light of publicity. It has been said of the rationale for disclosure that a public armed with knowledge about political contributions will be able to punish candidates who sell their office or who are otherwise inappropriately influenced.[109] Irrespective of the actual merits of this proposition, there can be no doubt that a well-informed public is better placed to appreciate the true extent and scope of postelectoral favors, and to draw appropriate conclusions from them, than one that is not.

The overriding interest the courts have cited to justify strict regulation of campaign contribution limits is the interest in preventing corruption or the appearance of corruption in the political process. This interest is no doubt a valid consideration in the case of direct contributions to political campaigns. In the case of some of the other more indirect contributions that political campaigns have attracted in recent years, its relevance is somewhat questionable. Based, at least in part, on concerns about the need to protect political speech, there has been some reluctance to regulate the so-called independent expenditures, or expenditures made without prearrangement or coordination with a candidate, expenditures incurred by political parties for party-building purposes, or expenditures in respect of the now infamous issue advertisements. Not surprisingly, independent expenditures, party-building, activities and issue advocacy have all come to be regarded as convenient instruments to be used to channel funds indirectly into political campaigns. Many of the allegations that have surfaced as a result of the last U.S. presidential campaign are linked to the use of one or other of these instruments.

That is not to suggest that these loopholes in campaign finance legislation cannot be fixed. There have been persistent calls for the appointment of an independent counsel to investigate alleged breaches of campaign finance legislation during the last presidential election. More importantly, there has been a campaign reform bill under consideration during the last Congress to address some of these issues. The McCain-Feingold Bill,[110] named after its two principal sponsors, seeks in effect to reform campaign finance legislation by narrowing the scope of some of the loopholes that have been used to circumvent campaign finance regulation.[111]

France. In France, campaign finance is governed by the French Electoral Code.[112] As in the case of FECA, the French Electoral Code regulates not only campaign expenditures but also campaign contribution limits. There are also strict disclosure requirements.

The French Electoral Code provides a ceiling for campaign expenditures, which varies according to the size of the population and the type of election,[113] as well as a series of rules and restrictions governing campaign contributions. It prescribes, among other things, a ceiling of FF30,000 on campaign donations provided by any individual for the benefit of one or more candidates at any election.[114] The code also bans campaign contributions in favor of any candidate by entities other than political parties and political groups, whether in the form of donations or in the form of goods or services, or any other benefit or advantage, direct or indirect, provided on terms that are more favorable than would normally apply.[115] There is a

limit on cash contributions to political campaigns,[116] as well as a requirement to have checks issued in respect of all donations in excess of FF1,000.[117]
As in the United States, there is a ban on foreign contributions, but only
with respect to contributions provided by foreign states and foreign entities.[118] Curiously enough, contributions by foreign individuals appear to
be exempt from the ban.

Although the French Electoral Code does not provide any comprehensive definition of campaign expenditures, as FECA does, there is nonetheless extensive jurisprudence available in France on the scope and extent of
such expenditures. The French courts have tended to treat as campaign
expenditures all expenditures incurred primarily to promote a candidate
and further his election. Conversely, expenditures incurred primarily for
a purpose other than the election are not treated as campaign expenditures, even if they may have indirectly served the candidate's interests in
the election process.[119] Thus, transport and communications costs, the costs
of publication of campaign materials, and office rent and personnel expenditures, including even the salaries of a candidate's security guards,
have all been treated as campaign expenditures to be accounted for in
election returns.[120] Conversely, general issue advertisements,[121] mailing
expenditures incurred by an official for purely routine administrative purposes,[122] and general party expenditures incurred for party-building purposes[123] have not been treated as campaign expenditures. More
interestingly, the courts seem willing to treat as campaign expenditures
those incurred for the benefit of a candidate by another, fictitious candidate,[124] or even by third parties acting with the candidate's consent, albeit
tacit.[125]

Finally, the French Electoral Code provides for campaign returns to be
prepared and submitted to the *Commission nationale des comptes de campagne
et des financements politiques* for its approval. This commission reserves the
right to approve or reject the returns or to approve them subject to
changes.[126] Breaches of the spending limits provided under the code call
for pecuniary sanctions and are referred to an election judge for a ruling.[127] Other breaches of the code are referred to the state prosecutor's
office for action.[128]

Conclusion. Campaign finance regulation is a formidable undertaking; but it is also an indispensable tool in the combat against corruption.
As recent experience with campaign finance regulation in the United States
shows, much remains to be done to plug some of the loopholes that have
been used to circumvent campaign finance legislation. That is not to say
that other countries have fared any better than the United States in the
application of campaign finance regulation. The United States, like France,
has adopted as sophisticated a set of campaign finance rules as any. The
fact that these rules have generated one scandal after another is not neces-

sarily indicative of a higher level of corruption than in other countries. Rather, it is evidence of a greater willingness on the part of the United States and France to recognize and address some of the pernicious effects of excessive and unregulated campaign contributions.

Regulated or not, campaign contributions are a potential source of corruption. In the United States, campaign finance reform is still very much alive. It is not by brushing the issue aside or sweeping it under the carpet, as many other countries have done, that the integrity of the political process can be maintained. The absence of major campaign finance-related scandals in many of those other countries is not so much an indication of a corruption-free political environment in those countries, as it is a reflection of the lack of transparency and public accountability that characterizes the electoral process and permeates the conduct of their public affairs.[129] The emerging democracies in the developing countries have useful lessons to draw from the French and U.S. experiences, and they have much to do in this difficult and formidable area to regulate.

Procurement

Introduction. Procurement, like campaign finance, is another major source of corruption. Admittedly, some countries are more vulnerable than others to charges of mismanagement of their public procurement activities. Although some countries have responded to the challenge by adopting reasonably effective and transparent procurement procedures, others have continued to be beset by one procurement scandal after another.

Public procurement activities in many countries continue to be tainted with fraud and corruption, and invariably saddled with protests, allegations of impropriety, and even court challenges. In some cases, the alleged irregularities result from a genuine lack of understanding of procurement rules and practices among officials. More frequently, however, they are attributable to weaknesses in the legal framework governing public procurement, which, in many cases, could have been avoided but for a simple, if somewhat ironic, fact of life: those who are vested with the power to introduce change are often the ones who are best served by the status quo. Not surprisingly, there have been repeated attempts to link at least some of the irregularities noted in public procurement activities with political campaign contributions. Hence, the inevitable link between procurement and campaign finance legislation.

Recent Legal Developments. Ever since procurement activities have been recognized as a potential source of corruption, many countries have set out in earnest to strengthen the legal framework governing their public procurement activities. A prime example is South Africa, whose constitution specifically refers to the need for a fair, equitable, transparent, competitive, and cost-effective system of public procurement.[130] In France, the *Code des marchés publics*[131] was updated on successive occasions in the early 1990s to improve the systems for public procurement. The *Code des marchés publics* is a comprehensive piece of legislation governing public contracts, including full details of procurement procedures, price and other financial clauses, dispute settlement clauses, and other contract provisions. In 1992, the Republic of Mali adopted a presidential decree[132] governing public contracts that closely follows the French model.

The United Nations Commission on International Trade Law (UNCITRAL) recently prepared a model law on the procurement of goods, construction, and services, which has since been adopted by the commission and issued by the United Nations.[133] This decision to undertake the preparation of a model law was, according to the "Guide to Enactment" annexed to the model law, made in response to the fact that in a number of countries, the governing procurement law is inadequate or outdated.[134] The model law is intended to serve as a model for states for the evaluation and modernization of their procurement laws and practices and for the establishment of procurement legislation where none presently exists.[135] The Republic of Latvia is one of the first countries to have put together a draft law on procurement based on the UNCITRAL model.[136]

The modern tendency is to have the legal framework governing procurement adopted by the legislative branch or, in the case of francophone states, by a decree issued by the *Chef d'Etat* or *chef de gouvernement*.[137] There are still countries, however, particularly those of Anglo-Saxon tradition, that continue to rely on so-called tender board regulations issued, usually, by the minister of finance, to govern public procurement. Such regulations are still in force in Kenya and in Ghana. In Mauritius, tender board regulations have been superseded by the adoption of the Central Tender Board Act,[138] which establishes the central tender board and prescribes its administrative functions and structure, but without prescribing either the basic principles or detailed rules governing procurement.

There are many considerations related to principles of openness, transparency, and fairness that have prompted countries to adopt legislation, and not mere administrative regulations, to govern procurement. Legislation, unlike a regulation, provides a reasonable guarantee that the rules of the game will not be changed arbitrarily or to suit particular situations or individuals. This is clearly the approach favored by the UNCITRAL model. By using its constitution to lay out its basic procurement principles, South Africa has sent a strong signal, to both its own nationals and to the international community, of the importance that it attaches to these basic principles. Conversely, countries that continue to rely on ministerial regulations for guidance in procurement matters send the opposite message: they agree to be bound by the rules, but only to the extent that their own interests continue to be served by those rules.

Purpose of Procurement Legislation. According to the UNCITRAL model, the purpose of procurement legislation is to maximize competition, accord fair treatment to suppliers and contractors, and enhance transparency and objectivity, and, in so doing, promote economy and efficiency and curb abuses.[139] In Madagascar, according to the explanatory note that accompanied the presentation of the relevant decree,[140] the purpose of the decree was to foster economy and efficiency, in terms of the rational use of public funds and competitive prices, and to promote domestic business, having regard to principles of fairness, transparency and nondiscrimination.[141] Similar sentiments are to be found in the procurement laws of many other countries.

The World Bank has its own set of procurement guidelines governing the procurement of goods and works under contracts financed by the Bank in its member countries.[142] The four considerations that guide the Bank procurement guidelines are, first, the need for economy and efficiency; second, the Bank's interest in giving all eligible bidders an equal opportunity to compete for Bank-financed contracts; third, the Bank's interest in encouraging the development of domestic contracting and manufacturing industries in the borrowing country; and, fourth, the importance of transparency in the procurement process.[143]

The underlying theme common to procurement laws in general is the need to promote economy and efficiency, as well as appropriate standards of transparency and accountability, while curbing abuse.

Choice of Procurement Method. Most legal systems have introduced competitive bidding as the method best suited to achieve the overall objectives of procurement legislation. Competitive bidding can be international or limited to national bidders; it can be open or restricted to a limited number of bidders, whether on the basis of prequalification or otherwise.[144] Even though international competitive bidding is presented as the preferred method of procurement, alternative methods may be appropriate in specified circumstances. Thus, under the model law, in cases of low-value procurement of standardized goods or services, it may be best to use the request-for-quotations method, which allows the procuring entity to solicit quotations from a limited number of suppliers and select the lowest-priced responsive offer.[145] In other circumstances, single-source procurement may be warranted.[146]

Whether the procurement entity decides to use competitive bidding or some other method of procurement, it is necessary to ensure that the procedures are appropriate and consistently applied with regard to the relevant provisions of the law. Any exception to the rule that competitive bidding is the norm must be fully justified and, if need be, approved by a higher authority.[147] The model law requires the procuring entity to keep a record of procurement proceedings, giving details of key decisions pertaining to the proceedings, including, in cases where a procurement method other than competitive bidding has been used, the grounds and circumstances on which the procuring entity relies to use such method.[148] Similarly, in cases where the procurement proceedings are limited to nationals, the record must indicate the grounds and circumstances relied upon by the procuring entity to impose such a limitation.[149] The purpose of such a record is quite clearly to promote transparency and accountability, and preempt possible abuses or perceptions of impropriety in the procurement process.

Bidders' Qualifications. Procurement rules generally include provisions to ensure that suppliers and contractors to whom public contracts are ultimately awarded have the necessary qualifications to provide the goods or services or execute the construction works, which are the subject matter of contracts. The model law, accordingly, requires suppliers and contractors to demonstrate that they have the necessary qualifications, including the professional qualifications and experience, technical competence and know-how, and the required financial and other resources, to perform their contracts.[150] Details of such qualifications must be specified in the bidding documents.[151] The model law goes on to provide that the prequalifications requirements as set forth in the bidding documents shall apply equally to all bidders, and that they shall constitute the sole basis for the evaluation of the qualifications of bidders.[152] In the case of complex contracts or assignments, there are also provisions for prequalification proceedings.[153]

Similar provisions are found in the national legislation of other countries. In France, the *Code des marchés publics* provides for details of the required qualifications to be specified in the bidding documents.[154] Based on the qualifications criteria specified in the bid documents, bidders are required to include appropriate evidence of their qualifications in an outer envelope accompanying their bids.[155] Unless they produce adequate evidence of their qualifications in the outer envelope, the inner envelope containing their actual bids is returned to them unopened. The procuring entity is precluded from using qualifications criteria other than those specified in the bidding documents to disqualify bidders.[156]

The rules governing bidders' qualifications serve a fundamental purpose. They contribute to a climate of fairness and transparency by ensuring that no participant in a procurement exercise can be eliminated except on grounds that have been communicated in advance to all bidders and apply across the board, without any discrimination on grounds of nationality or otherwise. The rules apply to all public contracts, whether they are awarded on the basis of competitive bidding or otherwise.

Submission of Bids. The key features of tender procedures are to be found in the UNCITRAL model law and summarized in its Guide to Enactment.[157] They include the need to give as wide publicity as may be appropriate to the invitation to bid, having regard to whether the tender is intended to be open or limited, local or international;[158] the need for a comprehensive description of the goods, construction works, and services that will be procured to be provided in the bid documents, along with detailed specifications, if any;[159] the need for full disclosure to suppliers and contractors of the criteria to be used in evaluating and comparing tenders and in selecting the successful tender;[160] and public opening of tenders.[161]

Bid submission procedures usually require the procuring entity to allow sufficient time for bidders to prepare and submit bids. Where, on its own initiative or as a result of a query or a request for clarification submitted by a bidder, the procuring entity issues a clarification or modification of the bidding documents, the procuring entity is required to communicate the clarification or modification to other potential bidders to whom the bidding documents have been provided, and, if necessary, extend the deadline for submission of bids to allow sufficient time for bids to be prepared and submitted.[162] Bids must be submitted in writing or in any other form specified in the bidding documents, which offers adequate guarantees of authenticity, security, and confidentiality.[163] As a rule, bids are opened in the presence of all bidders who have submitted bids, or their representatives, who wish to be present.[164]

The bid submission procedures have a common objective. They provide a common basis to suppliers and contractors for the preparation of bids, thus affording them an equal opportunity to compete for public contracts. In so doing, they seek to create the necessary conditions of honesty, fair play, and transparency needed to foster competition and promote economy and efficiency.

Evaluation Criteria. As in the case of qualifications criteria, basic procurement principles require all bid evaluation criteria to be specified in the bidding documents. Evaluation criteria may be based on price alone; more usually, however, they are based on a combination of price and other technical or economic factors.[165] It is provided in the model law that the bid documents must include criteria to be used in determining the successful tender, including any margin of preference and any nonprice criteria and the relative weight of such criteria.[166] The criteria to be used in the evaluation and comparison of bids are solely those specified in the bid documents.[167]

In case it is proposed to grant a preference in favor of domestic contractors or suppliers of goods or services, the margin of preference has to be determined and specified in the bidding documents, along with the applicable eligibility criteria for the grant of the preference.[168] In such cases, the margin of preference is treated as one more element in the list of evaluation criteria. Subject to the application of the margin of preference, the rules do not allow for further preferential treatment in favor of domestic contractors and suppliers.

The bid evaluation and comparison phase is one of the most critical phases of the procurement process. Its purpose is to determine the lowest evaluated bid, according to a common set of clear and objective evaluation criteria specified in the bid documents. The model law refers to the need to have evaluation criteria that are, to the extent practicable, "objective and quantifiable"[169]. Having objective and quantifiable evaluation criteria establishes a common basis for the evaluation and comparison of bids, and, in so doing, promotes objectivity and predictability and reduces the scope for arbitrary or discretionary decisions. In the context of the bid evaluation and comparison phase, arbitrariness and discretionary powers are a recipe for corruption.

Award of Contracts. The general rule is that the contract award has to be made in favor of the lowest evaluated bidder who meets the qualifications requirements and satisfies the other requirements specified in the bid documents. Negotiations with bidders on the terms of their respective bids, after the closing of bids and prior to the award, are not allowed. It is not unheard of for corrupt officials to engage in simultaneous negotiations with two or more of the highest ranked bidders on the price or other elements of their bid proposals in a deliberate attempt to reverse the final outcome of the bidding process. This is clearly an abuse of the procurement process. It is generally part of a scheme to use elements of the bid proposal of one bidder to apply pressure on another bidder in a disingenuous attempt to bring that other bidder to improve the terms of his own original bid.

The model law has a clear provision prohibiting negotiations between the procuring entity and a supplier or contractor concerning a tender submitted by the supplier or contractor.[170] To assist in the examination, evaluation, and comparison of bids, at the time of bid opening, a procuring entity has the right to ask suppliers or contractors for clarification of their tenders.[171] The entity may also, if need be, correct purely arithmetical errors discovered during the examination of bids.[172] The entity has no right, however, to make any change in a matter of substance in the bid, including changes in price or other changes aimed at making an unresponsive bid responsive.[173] Similar provisions are found in the Mali *Décret portant règlementation des marchés publics*, which requires the procuring entity to award the contract to the lowest evaluated bidder, with regard to the evaluation criteria specified in the bid documents.[174]

In addition, it is not unheard of for officials to decide after the fact to split a contract *among* more than one bidder, even though there is no provision to that effect in the bid documents. Again, this is clearly an abuse of the bidding process. In many cases, it represents an attempt by officials to frustrate the results of the bidding exercise, but without seeking to antagonize the would-be successful bidder to the point of risking an outright challenge of the process. Under the model law, the procuring entity is precluded from splitting the procurement as it sees fit after the fact, unless there is provision for split procurement in the bid documents.[175] In this connection, the Mali *Décret portant règlementation des marchés publics* provides that, whenever a contract is likely to be split or divided into lots, provision to that effect has to appear in the bid documents.[176]

The rules governing contract award are frequently disregarded by decisionmakers and other unscrupulous officials who have no immediate interest in a fair and transparent procurement process. The adoption of clear, objective, and transparent rules are an important safeguard to combat such practices, and create a climate of confidence and predictability, which is also one of the underlying objectives of procurement legislation in general.

World Bank-financed Contracts. Responding to concerns about the incidence of corruption in World Bank-financed contracts in its member countries, the World Bank took a series of initiatives recently to amend its procurement guidelines to address such concerns. A first set of amendments approved in July 1996 empowers the Bank to cancel an amount of the loan if it determines, with respect to any contract to be financed out of the proceeds of the loan, that the borrower's representatives or a beneficiary of the loan has engaged in corrupt or fraudulent practices during procurement activities or contract execution, and the borrower has failed to take timely and appropriate action to the Bank's satisfaction to remedy the situation. The same set of amendments also allows the Bank to reject a proposal for contract award if it determines that the bidder proposed for the award has engaged in corrupt or fraudulent practices in competing for the contract. Finally, the amendments also allow the Bank to blacklist bidders, contractors and suppliers, either indefinitely or for a stated period of time, if it determines that they have engaged in corrupt or fraudulent practices in competing for, or in executing, a Bank-financed contract.

Another amendment to the procurement guidelines approved in July 1997 permits the introduction of a so-called no-bribery clause, pursuant to which, for purposes of Bank-financed contracts, every bidder competing for or executing a contract undertakes to observe the country's laws against fraud and corruption.

The World Bank is currently engaged in a high profile campaign to combat corruption in its member countries. The amendments to the procurement guidelines were part and parcel of this current campaign. The emphasis that the Bank has placed on procurement activities in the course of its anti-corruption campaign provides a strong indication not just of the perceived links between procurement and corruption, but, more importantly, of the growing relevance of procurement rules and practices in the current debate on corruption.

III

Legal Framework to Combat Corruption—A Curative Approach

After a review of the so-called preventive laws, rules, and behavioral codes designed to promote a corruption-free environment, this section examines the contents of corruption laws and their application. It deals, successively, with the process of investigation of corruption offenses and the judicial process, including the special rules of evidence, and sanctions and penalties, applicable to corruption offenses.

Investigation of Corruption

Traditional Enforcement Mechanisms

The decision to charge an accused person with a criminal offense, or to investigate a suspect for an economic crime or any other crime, is a serious matter and one that ought not to be treated lightly. Surprisingly, the seriousness with which this issue is treated varies from one jurisdiction to another. In most Anglo-Saxon jurisdictions, such decisions are taken by either the police or the prosecutor's office, depending on the nature and gravity of the offense. This is not the case in the United States or France.

France. In France, the decision to open a criminal investigation and charge an accused person with a crime is taken invariably by investigating magistrates (*juges d'instruction*) appointed by the courts. The investigating magistrate is appointed at the request of the state prosecutor's office or a complainant. The role of the *juge d'instruction* is not to seek an indictment at all costs, but to gather evidence pertaining to a crime and determine whether there is sufficient evidence to indict an accused and, if so, to refer the case to the appropriate tribunal. In this process, the *juge d'instruction* has powers to hear witnesses, search premises, appoint expert witnesses, and, if necessary, issue summonses to witnesses and warrants of arrest. He can call on both the police and the state prosecutor's office for assistance, as needed. The *juge d'instruction* is also competent to make an order for the detention of the accused party or to rule on an application for the accused's release pending the outcome of the investigation. The decision of the *juge d'instruction* to indict or not to indict the accused party, as the case may be, is subject to a final appeal to the *chambre d'accusation* of the court of appeal.

Several reasons account for the weight accorded to the indictment decision in France and other similar jurisdictions. First, a decision to charge an accused party for an offense has the potential to cause irreparable harm to the accused's reputation, because of the negative publicity that it generates, particularly in cases where the accused party is a prominent personality. Even in cases where the charges are subsequently dismissed, it comes as little consolation to those involved to discover that a dismissal seldom attracts as much publicity as an original indictment. Second, in cases where the accused is an employee, a decision to charge him with a criminal offense, irrespective of the final outcome, is bound to have adverse effects on his continued employment and career prospects. Third, there are, inevitably, many instances in which an indictment is followed by an order for the preventive detention of the accused party. Quite apart from any stigma that such an order never fails to generate, its consequences are invariably damaging for both the accused and the accused's family.

The United Kingdom and Other Anglo-Saxon Jurisdictions. In most Anglo-Saxon jurisdictions, the police, not judicial personnel, is invariably in charge of criminal investigations. In the United Kingdom, the consent of the Attorney General or the Director of Public Prosecutions (DPP) is required for the prosecution of specific offenses. Similarly, the Crown Prosecution Service (CPS), which is headed by the DPP, has the discretion to prosecute or stop proceedings. It may also ask the police to investigate criminal offenses, but cannot order it to do so. More important, the CPS has no authority to supervise police investigations.[177] Even in cases where the decision to indict the accused is taken by the prosecutor's office, the decision is bound to be strongly colored by the outcome of the police investigation, to the point of being, in many cases, a mere formality.

The inquisitorial process that characterizes the French system stands in sharp contrast with the more adversarial process of the Anglo-Saxon system, the outcome of which depends on the outcome of the exchanges between the parties before the court. There are rare cases of serious crimes in which a preliminary investigation is required as a matter of law before criminal proceedings can be instituted. Except for such cases, the decision to institute criminal proceedings is never subject to any prior judicial control, as in France. In cases where an accused party's contention is that there is no *prima facie* case made out and that, accordingly, there is no case to answer, the only remedy available to the accused is to make a submission to that effect, but only at the trial, and then only after the prosecution has rested its case.

The United States. In the United States, as in France, the authority of the District Attorney (DA) to file charges in felony cases is invariably subject to a process of pretrial judicial scrutiny. As in other Anglo-Saxon jurisdictions, the police conducts investigations and recommends charges. However, although the DA is competent to file charges, he is not free to refer felony cases to a superior court until either a lower court or a grand jury, if there is one, has certified that there is sufficient evidence on record to convict the defendant. The grand jury is a group of citizens convened by the court, whose role is to decide whether there is sufficient evidence to charge a person with a felony and, if so, to indict him accordingly. The grand jury has broad investigative powers; but its proceedings are secret.

General. It is no wonder that, as corruption reached unprecedented levels and there were mounting calls for action to contain it, countries such as the United States and France were fully prepared to meet the challenge. In both of these countries, it was business as usual, even as independent-minded investigators on both sides of the Atlantic proceeded relentlessly to investigate corruption allegations involving the highest echelons of the executive branch. Other countries that did not share the same strong tradition of investigative independence, including countries that had inherited the French legal system but without the same respect for judicial independence, had little to offer, except more of the same, in terms of charges and allegations involving previous regimes and opposition groups.

In many of these countries, their ill-trained and poorly educated police forces— riddled, in many cases, with corruption in their own midst—had already had the limits of their investigative powers tested by routine criminal investigations. Lacking in both the necessary sophistication and technical know-how, they were ill prepared to cope with the additional challenge of investigating corruption and other economic crimes. It would not be long before their inability to combat economic crime, coupled with an overriding public need to demonstrate commitment to combating corruption, would generate a demand for the establishment of specialized enforcement agencies, skilled in the art of investigating white-collar crime and specially trained to penetrate its sophisticated world. Not surprisingly, the creation of politically controlled specialized agencies, directly answerable to the executive branch and sympathetic to its political agenda, would also, in many cases, serve as a powerful political tool to discredit political opponents.

The U.S. Independent Counsel

The United States, which has had its own "Watergate" and other major scandals involving the presidential administrations to contend with, was quick to recognize that an administration cannot credibly investigate itself. Any attempt to have a key member of the administration investigated by the Attorney General has been viewed with skepticism, not least because of the perception of a conflict of interest that it creates. Even a finding that happens to clear the administration of any wrongdoing, no matter how much it is substantiated, tends to enhance public skepticism about the credibility of the investigative process.

It was precisely to avoid this appearance of a conflict of interest that the independent counsel process was established in the aftermath of the Watergate scandal. The Independent Counsel Statute[178] was promulgated as part of the Ethics in Government Act of 1978.[179] It was part of an overall attempt by lawmakers to prevent abuses of presidential power, create and reorganize agencies of the federal government, and enhance the probity of public officials and institutions.[180] The statute applies to investigations concerning the president and vice president of the United States, cabinet members, officials of the Department of Justice, and other senior officials of the administration, as well as individuals who have previously occupied such offices or positions[181] and members of Congress.[182]

According to the statute, whenever the Attorney General receives information suggesting that there are grounds to investigate whether such an official may have committed an offense under a federal criminal law, he is required to conduct a preliminary investigation with a view to determining whether further investigation of the official by an independent counsel is warranted.[183] The Attorney General has a time limit of 30 days after receiving such information within which to determine whether there are sufficient grounds for a preliminary investigation.[184] Unless the Attorney General is able within the 30-day period to make a positive determination to the effect that the information is not sufficiently specific or the source insufficiently credible, the statute requires him to proceed with a preliminary investigation.[185]

The statute prescribes a deadline of 90 days after the beginning of the preliminary investigation,[186] within which the Attorney General is required to file a notification to the appropriate division of the court. If the Attorney General determines that there are no reasonable grounds to believe that further investigation is warranted, he may decide to bring the process to a close.[187] Alternatively, if the Attorney General determines that there are grounds to believe that further investigation is warranted, or even if no notification is filed within the specified time frame, the court is required to proceed with the appointment of an independent counsel.[188] Unless a preliminary investigation can show conclusively that an allegation is false, the Attorney General must seek an independent counsel.

Subject to the prosecutorial jurisdiction of the Office of the Independent Counsel, the independent counsel has extensive investigative and prosecutorial powers to conduct proceedings before grand juries and other investigations, participate in court proceedings and engage in any litigation that he considers necessary, review documentary evidence, and start and conduct prosecutions in any court of competent jurisdiction in the name of the United States.[189] The independent counsel reports to Congress[190] and cannot be removed from office except for good cause.[191]

Independent counsels have been appointed to investigate a number of politically charged complaints. Many such investigations have been criticized on the grounds that they tend to be costly, protracted, and partisan. In the aftermath of the negative public reaction to the recent impeachment proceedings against President Clinton, there is growing speculation that Congress may not renew the Independent Counsel Statute when it expires on June 30, 1999. Not surprisingly, much of the criticism leveled at the independent counsel has tended to be as partisan as the investigations themselves.[192]

Notwithstanding the existence of such controversial investigations, the independent counsel process has gone a long way toward isolating the appointment of independent counsel from politics, emphasizing the legal considerations that drive the appointment process at the expense of purely political considerations. It is interesting to note that the decision to apply for the appointment of an independent counsel is the Attorney General's alone, and it is not subject to a challenge before any court of law. Such a decision is not intended to amount to an indictment or to raise any presumption of guilt or wrongdoing on the part of officials under investigation. At best, it is intended to be the expression of the Attorney General's determination that there are grounds to believe that further investigation is warranted. There have been cases in which independent counsels have been appointed amid strong evidence of criminal conduct. There has also been at least one case in recent months in which Attorney General Janet Reno sought the appointment of an independent counsel, not so much because she believed that there was evidence to warrant a prosecution, but because she was convinced that the law left her no other choice.[193]

A special counsel, according to one commentator, may sometimes be the only way to investigate the executive branch, especially at the highest levels. The Department of Justice may be too compromised; Congress, whose job this should be in principle, is sometimes too partisan.[194] The impending demise of the Independent Counsel Statute, if indeed it is confirmed, is bound to be followed by further calls for an investigative process independent of the Department of Justice to investigate crimes involving elected and other senior officials of the executive branch.

Other Specialized Corruption Investigation Agencies

Partly to mitigate the shortcomings of the adversarial investigative procedure, and partly in recognition of the limited capability of conventional
police forces, many countries have opted for specialized corruption investigation agencies of their own to investigate and combat economic crimes
and corruption in particular. Hong Kong established its Independent Commission against Corruption (ICAC). Tanzania and Malawi established the
Prevention of Corruption Bureau and the Anti-Corruption Bureau, respectively. Similar agencies have been established in Singapore, Pakistan,
Kenya, and Mauritius.

Hong Kong. ICAC was established by the Independent Commission
against Corruption Ordinance (Chapter 204). It consists of a commissioner, a deputy commissioner, and such other officers as may be appointed.[195] Both the commissioner and deputy commissioner are
appointed by the chief executive. The commissioner is answerable to
the chief executive in the exercise of his functions under the ordinance,
but he is not otherwise subject to the direction or control of any other
person.[196] The role of ICAC is to receive and investigate allegations of
corruption, including alleged or suspected offenses under the ordinance
and related legislation, including the Prevention of Bribery Ordinance
(Cap. 201, 14 May 1971, Law No. 58 of 1971, originally 102 of 1970) and
Corrupt and Illegal Practices Ordinance, as well as alleged or suspected
offenses of blackmail involving public officials or misuse of public office.[197] The commission is also competent to examine the practices and
procedures of government departments with a view to facilitating the
discovery of corrupt practices and securing the revision of work methods and procedures, as well as advising on changes in practices and
procedures needed to reduce the likelihood of occurrence of corrupt practices.

Singapore. The Corrupt Practices Investigation Bureau (CPIB) is an independent body that investigates and seeks to prevent corruption in the
public and private sectors in Singapore. Established in 1952, it derives its
powers of investigation from the Prevention of Corruption Act (Chapter
241, Statutes, Law of 1952, 1993 revision). The bureau is headed by a director who is directly answerable to the Prime Minister.

The CPIB is responsible for safeguarding the integrity of the public service and encouraging corruption-free transactions in the private sector. It
is also charged with the responsibility of checking on malpractices by public
officers and reporting such cases to the appropriate government departments and public bodies for disciplinary action. Although the primary
function of the bureau is to investigate corruption under the Prevention of
Corruption Act, it is also empowered to investigate any other arrestable

offense under any written law that is disclosed in the course of a corruption investigation.

Besides bringing corruption offenders to book, the CPIB carries out activities aimed at preventing corruption. For example, it reviews the work methods and procedures of corruption-prone departments and public bodies to identify administrative weaknesses in the existing systems that could facilitate corruption and malpractices, and it recommends remedial and preventive measures to the heads of departments concerned. CPIB officers regularly conduct lectures and seminars to educate public officers, especially those who come into contact with the public, on the pitfalls of—and the avoidance of—corruption.

Pakistan. In Pakistan, the Accountability Ordinance provides the legal and institutional framework to combat corruption. The ordinance provides for the establishment of a Chief Ehtesab Commission (CEC), headed by a commissioner, to investigate allegations of corruption and corrupt practices, and institute proceedings accordingly before a bench of three High Court judges.[198]The commissioner, who has the rank of a Supreme Court judge, is appointed for a term of four years. The appointment of CEC officers and staff is made by the federal government with the concurrence of the CEC. The CEC is vested with wide-ranging powers, including the power to seek the required assistance and call for documents and information relevant to any proceedings pending before it, and the power to punish for contempt.

The Accountability Ordinance provides effective measures for prosecution and speedy disposal of cases involving corruption and corrupt practices, including extraordinary powers of the court to order forfeiture of property obtained through corruption and corrupt practices and property found to be disproportionate to the known sources of income of the accused party, and power to freeze the property of an accused party, before a conviction, if the court has reasonable grounds to believe that the accused party has committed an offense.[199]

Tanzania. The Tanzanian Prevention of Corruption Bureau was established by the Tanzanian president pursuant to the Prevention of Corruption Act.[200] It consists of a director general and directors, and other officers as the president may determine. Its functions are to take measures to prevent corruption in the public, parastatal, and private sectors; investigate and prosecute for offenses involving corruption; and advise on ways to prevent corruption. The bureau is subject to the control and supervision of the president. In the exercise of its powers to prosecute for offenses under the Prevention of Corruption Act, it is also subject to the directions of the Director of Public Prosecutions.

Malawi. The Malawi Corrupt Practices Act of 1995 established the Anti-Corruption Bureau, which consists of a director, a deputy director, and such other officers as may be appointed from time to time.[201] The director is appointed by the president, but he is subject to the direction and control of the relevant government minister on all matters of policy, and the appointment is subject to confirmation by the Public Appointments Committee (PAC).[202] Both the director and deputy director are liable to be suspended or dismissed for cause by the president, subject, however, in the case of dismissal, to confirmation by the PAC.[203]

The powers and functions of the Anti-Corruption Bureau are not unlike those of its counterpart in Hong Kong.[204] It has extensive powers of arrest and search and seizure, as well as access to books, records, and other documents relevant to its functions.[205] As in the case of its counterparts in Hong Kong and Tanzania, it is also subject, in the exercise of its powers to prosecute for offenses under the act, to the directions of the Director of Public Prosecutions. Under certain circumstances, the Director is even empowered to issue an order directing an officer of the bureau to investigate any bank account, share account, purchase account, or any other account or safe deposit box in any bank, and the issue of such an order is deemed to be sufficient authority for the release by any person of any information or other document pertaining to such account or safe deposit box.[206]

Kenya. The role and functions of the Anti-Corruption Authority are governed by the Prevention of Corruption Act.[207] The Act gives the director of the Anti-Corruption Authority wide-ranging powers to investigate and prosecute offenses involving corruption.[208] It vests employees of the authority with powers similar to those of the police. In the performance of their functions, the members of the authority are vested with all the powers of a police officer of the rank of assistant superintendent of police. The provisions of the Police Act conferring upon police officers powers necessary for the prevention, investigation, and prosecution of offenses apply equally to them.

The Prevention of Corruption Act represents a bold move on the part of the authorities to provide the director with some degree of security of tenure and, in so doing, isolate the office from political interference. The conditions and circumstances in which the director can be removed from office are stated and prescribed in the Act. It is expressly provided that the director can be removed from office, but only if he is incapacitated, bankrupt, or convicted of a criminal offense, or if he absents himself from office. When it is intended to remove the director, the Act provides for the appointment of a tribunal of judges to investigate the allegations against him and make recommendations accordingly to the president.

Mauritius. The Unified Revenue Board in Mauritius was established pursuant to the Unified Revenue Act of 1993. The functions of the Unified Revenue Board are, among other things, to "co-ordinate and supervise the activities of the revenue departments,"[209] to "take such measures as may be necessary to improve the effectiveness of the revenue departments and maximize revenue collection in Mauritius,"[210] and to "determine the steps to be taken to counteract fraud and other forms of fiscal evasion."[211] Subject to the overall authority of the board, the Commissioner of Fiscal Investigations has authority to "take such steps as may be necessary with a view to expediting revenue collection or combating fraud and other forms of fiscal evasion."[212] In the discharge of its functions under the Act, the board is required to act in accordance with such directions of a general character as the minister may issue from time to time.[213] All the board's members either report to or are designated by the minister.[214]

General Observations. The Hong Kong model has been widely cited as a one of the rare success stories in the campaign against corruption. Its legislative framework has served as a model in many other countries, including Malawi and Botswana. Following the Hong Kong model, many countries in Africa and elsewhere have enacted new laws, established new specialized corruption investigative agencies, and defined new corruption-related offenses. To date, however, there is no hard evidence to suggest that the Hong Kong success story has been widely replicated abroad.

At least three elements account for the successful enforcement of corruption laws. First, an enforcement agency must have available adequate resources—human, physical, and intellectual—to be effective. Second, it has to be independent of the political leadership. Third, its actions can succeed only to the extent that they are matched by the requisite measure of political will to combat corruption. It is reasonable to assume that ICAC in Hong Kong has been blessed on all three counts. Where political will to combat corruption runs deep, it serves not only to strengthen the hand of the enforcement agency, but also to unleash the resources that it requires to deliver the goods.

The presence of these three elements—adequate resources, independence, and political will—may have contributed to yet another factor that accounts for the Hong Kong success story: the commitment of the people of Hong Kong to the rule of law.[215]

Corruption investigation is an expensive undertaking, requiring considerable resources and involving special skills and a level of professionalism that few developing countries care to develop. It also requires a delicate balance of political support and independence that is not always readily achievable. Beyond paying lip service to the need to eradicate corruption and engaging in a handful of mostly politically motivated anticorruption crusades by subservient watchdog agencies under their control, many political leaders have shied away from any genuine attempt to empower their enforcement agencies and provide them with both the resources and the independence they need to establish their credibility.

As examples from several developing countries readily demonstrate, there is still a strong tendency among political leaders in such countries to keep a tight control over the investigative process in corruption cases and, in so doing, make sure it never gets out of hand. The control model adopted has varied from one developing country to another. In some cases, a tight and highly centralized control model has been adopted, giving political leaders unrestricted authority to oversee both individual staffing arrangements and the progress of individual investigations. In other cases, the control model has been more relaxed, leaving it to enforcement agencies themselves to use their best judgment to conduct investigations and establish their findings, subject only to such general directives as the political leadership may issue from time to time.

Although there is no compelling reason to assume that political leaders are a main source of corrupt practices, let alone the only source, there is a real perception—at least in the eyes of the public—that, along with other public officials, they rank among the chief perpetrators of corruption offenses and other economic crimes, if only because of the power they wield and, more important, their ready access to public funds. To vest the same political leaders and their acolytes with day-to-day control over the investigation of corruption offenses is to subvert a quasi-investigative process and undermine its credibility, reducing it at best to a preferred instrument of political vendetta. In countries where democratic reforms have been accompanied by periodic changes of regime, political leaders would do well to remind themselves that successive regimes have been known to enforce—to equally damaging effect—the unjust laws and other reprehensible legal instruments they inherit from their predecessors, subverting them for their own political ends and, in the process, providing their predecessors with a proverbial taste of their own medicine.

Judicial Process

Traditional Bribery Legislation

In most countries, bribery legislation has been on the statute books for a long time. Well before bribery and corruption came to be regarded as special offenses requiring special treatment, there were already provisions in the legislation of most countries relating to offenses of bribery and corruption. Such provisions were usually to be found in the penal code and, in some cases, in special corruption legislation.

The United Kingdom. In the United Kingdom, the existing legislation governing the offense of bribery involving public officers dates back to an Act of Parliament introduced late in the 19th century.[216] The Act makes it an offense for any person to solicit or receive, or to give, promise, or offer,

to a public officer, any gift, loan, fee, reward, or advantage as an inducement or reward for any public officer to do, or refrain from doing, an act in
respect of any matter or transaction in which a public body is concerned.
Legislation governing acts of bribery in the private sector was introduced
in 1906.[217] Similar legislation governing corruption in both the public and
private sectors was introduced in Kenya in 1956.[218]

The United States. According to bribery legislation in the United States,
it is an offense for any person to give, offer, or promise directly or indirectly anything of value to any public official for or because of any official act performed or to be performed by such public official.[219] Conversely,
it is also an offense for such an official to demand, seek, receive, accept,
or agree to receive or accept anything of value personally for, or because
of, any official act performed or to be performed by such official.[220]. The
provisions do not apply obviously to cases in which the reward, gift, or
promise is made, offered, or given, or received or accepted by the official,
in accordance with the law and for the proper discharge of an official
duty.

France. In France, as in Mauritius, there are provisions in the penal code
governing bribery offenses. French law makes a distinction between active and passive acts of corruption. An active act of corruption is committed whenever any person gives or offers any gift, reward, or other
advantage to any public officer, to induce the officer to do, or to refrain
from doing, an act in the execution of his duties. Conversely, an act of
corruption is deemed to be passive whenever it is the officer who solicits
or receives a gift, reward, or other advantage in order to do, or to refrain
from doing, an act in the execution of his duties. In both cases, the act of
corruption is punishable under the penal code.[221]

Similarly, in Mauritius, it is an offense under the penal code for any
public officer to accept or receive a bribe, or for any person to give or offer
a bribe to such an officer, if the purpose of the bribe is to induce the officer
to do, or to refrain from doing, an act in the execution of his duties, or to
reward him on account of such an act done in the execution of his duties.[222]

Special Corruption Offenses

The United States. The Foreign Corrupt Practices Act was promulgated
in 1977. The Act makes it an offense for any company registered in the
United States; its employees or agents; any U.S. citizen, national, or resi-
dent; or any other U.S.-based enterprise to be involved in foreign corrupt
practices. For purposes of the Act, "foreign corrupt practices" involve the
use of mail or other means of interstate commerce to give, offer, or promise to any foreign official or political party or candidate for political office
anything of value to bring the foreign official, political party, or candidate

for political office to use his influence, directly or indirectly, to assist the company, enterprise, or individual to secure or retain business.[223]

The Foreign Corrupt Practices Act provides for an exception in the case of a payment to a foreign official, political party, or party official for the purpose of expediting or securing the performance of a so-called "routine governmental action."[224] Similarly, it is a defense under the Act that the payment, promise, or offer was lawful under the laws of the foreign country concerned, or that it was a reasonable and bona fide expenditure incurred for the promotion, demonstration, or explanation of products or services, or for the execution or performance of a contract with a foreign government or agency.[225]

The Foreign Corrupt Practices Act empowers the Attorney General to issue guidelines on standards of conduct that the Attorney General would regard as being in conformity with the Act.[226] At the request of concerned parties, the Attorney General may also issue advisory opinions, indicating whether and, if so, to what extent any prospective conduct of such parties is, in the Attorney General's view, consistent with the standards laid down in the Act. The Attorney General's advisory opinion is not binding on a court of law, but, in cases where the conduct under review had been supported by a favorable advisory opinion, such an opinion creates a rebuttable presumption that such conduct was indeed consistent with the Act.[227]

It has been suggested that the United States may be the only nation in the world that punishes criminally its business community for bribing another country's public servants. Whether this statement is strictly correct is questionable. Suffice it to say, however, that the enforcement record under the Foreign Corrupt Practices Act has been somewhat mixed, with convictions few and far between.[228] There are several obvious reasons that account for the dubious record of the Act.

First and foremost, it is clearly not in the best interest of the United States to bring systematically charges of bribery of foreign officials against its own citizens while other states condone similar acts involving their own citizens. To do so would undermine the ability of U.S. companies and businesses to compete for business in other countries. Second, the Act suffers from a lack of clarity, which makes it difficult to determine in specific situations whether the conduct complained of amounts to a breach of the Act or not. Third, even if a specific form of conduct is determined to be actionable under the Act, charges of bribery of foreign officials invariably involve complex and time-consuming investigations. Such investigations require significant resources that the United States, like any other country, may prefer to allocate to other, more visible law and order issues, such as violent crimes, drug-trafficking offenses, and other issues considered to be of higher priority.

Tanzania. The Tanzanian Prevention of Corruption Act creates three sets of corruption offenses. The first set relates to so-called corrupt transactions, which, unlike other offenses created under the Act, are not restricted to the public sector. The Tanzanian Prevention of Corruption Act makes it an offense for any person to corruptly solicit, accept, or obtain, or to agree to accept or attempt to obtain, any advantage as an inducement to, or reward for, doing or forbearing to do, or for having done or forborne to do, anything in relation to his principal's affairs or business.[229] A similar offense is created in respect of any person who corruptly gives, promises, or offers an advantage under similar circumstances.[230] This first set of offenses applies exclusively to cases in which the recipient or intended recipient of the advantage acts, not on his account, but on behalf of a principal. Although the offenses are not limited to transactions involving public officials, there are harsher penalties provided for offenses committed in relation to public sector contracts.[231]

The other two sets of offenses are limited to transactions involving public officials. In the first case, Tanzania's Prevention of Corruption Act makes it an offense for a public officer to solicit, accept, or obtain, or to agree to accept or attempt to obtain, any undue advantage from any person in connection with his official duties. The other set of offenses relates to the failure on the part of a public officer to satisfactorily account for wealth he may have or may have had in his possession, or for the benefit of services which he may have received.

Under the Act, the appropriate authorities are empowered by notice in writing to require any public officer to provide a full and true account of properties that such public officer may have or have had in his possession, including a true account of how such property has been acquired.[232] Failure to provide such a full and true account as required in the notice is in itself an offense punishable with imprisonment of up to two years.[233] Moreover, where a public officer is found to be or to have been in possession of property, or to have received the benefit of services, that he is reasonably suspected of having corruptly acquired or received while holding public office, he may be charged with an offense under the Act and required to satisfy a court of law that he did not corruptly acquire the property or receive the benefit of services, as the case may be; failing which, he may be deemed to have corruptly acquired the property or received the benefit of services, as the case may be.[234]

Malawi. Most of the offenses provided under the Tanzanian Prevention of Corruption Act are also to be found in the Malawi Corrupt Practices Act. As in Tanzania, the Corrupt Practices Act makes a distinction between corrupt transactions involving public officials and those that do not. Both types of transactions are covered under the Act and punished accordingly. Unlike the Tanzanian Act, however, the Malawi Corrupt Practices Act goes on to create a number of offenses relating to abuse of authority on the part of public officials and other persons in connection with the award of contracts.

It is an offense under the Act for a member of a public body to corruptly solicit, accept, or obtain, or to agree to accept or attempt to receive or obtain, or for any other person to corruptly give, promise, or offer to a member of a public body, any gratification as an inducement or reward for such member of a public body to use his voting rights or other influence to further or hinder any course of action, or to procure any contract or advantage in favor of any person.[235] Similarly, it is also an offense for any public officer to corruptly solicit, accept, or obtain, or to agree to accept or attempt to receive or obtain, or for any other person to corruptly give, promise, or offer to a public officer, any gratification as an inducement or reward for such public officer to exercise undue influence for the promotion, execution, or procurement of any contract involving a public or private body, or for the payment of any price, consideration, or other moneys thereunder.[236] Finally, it is an offense under the Act for any person to corruptly solicit, accept, or obtain, or to agree to accept or attempt to receive or obtain, or for any other person to corruptly give, promise, or offer to any such person, any gratification as an inducement or reward for the withdrawal of a tender or for refraining from making a tender for any contract with a public or private body,[237] or for refraining from making a bid at any sale by auction conducted by or on behalf of a public or private body.[238]

There are also provisions in the Malawi Corrupt Practices Act pertaining to a public officer who maintains a standard of living, or has pecuniary resources or property, that is not commensurate with his official emoluments, past or present, or other known sources of income, or is in receipt of the benefit of services which he is reasonably suspected of having received corruptly or under circumstances that may amount to an offense under the Act.[239] Although the Act does not appear to make it an offense as such for a public officer to maintain such a standard of living or to have such pecuniary resources or property, or to be in receipt of such benefit of services, it does require the officer, upon receipt of a notice in writing to that effect, to provide a satisfactory explanation of such standard of living, pecuniary resources or property, or receipt of the benefit of services, as the case may be.[240]

Finally, the Malawi Corrupt Practices Act, like the U.S. Foreign Corrupt Practices Act, claims to have extraterritorial application. Its provisions are declared to be applicable to citizens and residents of Malawi both within and outside Malawi, and offenses committed thereunder by such citizens and residents outside Malawi are treated and dealt with as if they had been committed within Malawi.[241] In view of the specific scope

52 COMBATING CORRUPTION

of the terms "public bodies" and "public officers," which have been defined under the Act to refer solely to public bodies and public officers of Malawi, it is reasonable to assume that offenses involving public bodies and public officers under the Act can only be committed in relation to such public bodies and public officers of Malawi. Even though the Act provides for extraterritorial jurisdiction, it is doubtful that Malawi, any more than the United States, has either the ability or the inclination to divert significant resources away from more pressing domestic concerns to engage in the aggressive pursuit of acts of bribery committed outside its immediate borders.

Hong Kong. In Hong Kong, the provisions governing bribery of public officials are not found in the law creating the special corruption law enforcement agency, but in a separate Prevention of Bribery Act.[242] The main focus of the Act is on acts of bribery involving public officials. The Act makes it an offense for any person, whether in Hong Kong or elsewhere and without lawful authority or reasonable excuse, to offer any advantage to a public servant. The Act also makes it an offense for a public servant to solicit or accept such an advantage if the purpose thereof is to induce or reward any act or omission on the part of the public servant, or to favor any person or put him at a disadvantage.[243]

Hong Kong's Prevention of Bribery Act defines an advantage as including any service or favor accruing to the public servant.[244] It places the burden of proving lawful authority or reasonable excuse on the accused.[245]. In any proceedings under the Act, it is not a defense to show that any advantage is customary in any profession, trade, vocation, or calling.[246] As in the case of the U.S. Foreign Corrupt Practices Act and the Malawi Corrupt Practices Act, the Hong Kong Prevention of Bribery Act claims to have extraterritorial jurisdiction to the extent that the offense of bribery can be committed "whether in Hong Kong or elsewhere." In this case, however, the extraterritorial nature of the jurisdiction is limited to the extent that the alleged bribery has to relate to a public servant of Hong Kong.[247]

As in the case of Malawi, there are provisions pertaining to bribes offered or solicited as an inducement or reward for the promotion, execution. or procurement of any contract, or for the payment of any price, consideration, or other moneys thereunder,[248] for the withdrawal of a tender or for refraining from making a tender for any contract,[249] or for refraining from making a bid at any sale by auction,[250] but only in cases of contracts and auctions involving a public body. The Act also makes provisions in relation to corrupt transactions with agents acting on behalf of their principals.[251]

Finally, as in Tanzania, the Act makes it an offense for any public servant to either maintain a standard of living above that commensurate with, or to be in control of pecuniary resources or property disproportionate to, his present or past official emoluments, unless he can satisfactorily account for such a standard of living or pecuniary resources or property, as the case may be.[252] Where the pecuniary resources or other property that is the subject matter of the charge is held by a person other than the accused party, and the court is satisfied that that person was holding such pecuniary resources or property on trust for the accused or received such pecuniary resources or property as a gift from the accused, such pecuniary resources or property may, having regard to that person's relationship to the accused or other circumstances and in the absence of evidence to the contrary, be presumed to have been in the control of the accused.[253]

Where any person has been convicted on account of pecuniary resources or property in his control, which he has failed to satisfactorily account for, the court may, at the request of the Attorney General, and in addition to other penalties provided under the Act, make an order for the confiscation of pecuniary resources or property in his control, not exceeding the amount or value of pecuniary resources or property that the convicted party failed to satisfactorily account for.[254] A confiscation order shall not be made in relation to pecuniary resources or property held by a person other than the convicted party, unless that other person has been given adequate notice of the proposed order and an opportunity to show cause why it should not be made,[255] or if that other person satisfies the court that he acted in good faith or that, in regard to the circumstances in which the pecuniary resources or property were acquired, an order would be unjust.[256]

Money Laundering

Money laundering is the process of transformation of the form or usage of ill-gotten proceeds of economic crimes, with a view to obscuring the source or origin of such proceeds. The term "money laundering" has traditionally been associated with drug-trafficking offenses. Today, however, money laundering has come to be regarded as an essential element in the fight against corruption. Its scope has been extended to apply generally to all economic crimes, including corruption offenses. As in the case of drug trafficking, the purpose of money laundering legislation is to ensure that crime does not pay, and that no amnesty is provided after the fact to perpetrators of serious economic crimes.

The United Kingdom. In the United Kingdom, legislation creating money-laundering offenses in connection with drug trafficking was first introduced in 1986.[257] But it was not until the Criminal Justice Act of 1993, amending the Criminal Justice Act of 1988, that money-laundering provisions were extended generally to cover other forms of criminal conduct. The Criminal Justice Act makes it an offense for any person to be involved in any arrangement designed to enable another person to retain control over the proceeds of criminal conduct, or to have such proceeds placed at that other person's disposal or applied to acquire property by way of investment on his behalf, knowing that that other person has been involved in criminal conduct or has benefited from criminal conduct.[258] In any proceedings against any person under the Act, it is a defense for the accused party to prove that he did not know or suspect that the arrangement related to the proceeds of criminal conduct or that the effect thereof was to enable that other person to retain control over the proceeds of criminal conduct, or to have such proceeds placed at that other person's disposal or applied to acquire property by way of investment on his behalf, or that he intended to disclose details pertaining to the arrangement, or that his failure to do so was excusable.[259] There are also provisions in the Act to protect the rights of persons involved in such arrangements who take appropriate steps to disclose the arrangements' existence to police or other persons in authority.[260]

Similarly, it is an offense for any person to conceal or disguise, for the purpose of avoiding prosecution, any property that is the proceeds of that person's own criminal conduct, or to convert or transfer such property out of the jurisdiction, or the making or enforcing of a confiscation order relating to such property.[261.] It is also an offense for any person to conceal or disguise any property that is the proceeds of another person's criminal conduct or to convert or transfer such property out of the jurisdiction, for the purpose of assisting that other person in avoiding prosecution, or the making or enforcing of a confiscation order relating to such property.[262]

Switzerland. Faced with criticism that its state-of-the-art financial services had combined with the absence of regulatory constraints and strict bank secrecy rules to make Switzerland a haven for the safekeeping of proceeds of criminal activities, Switzerland has taken a number of measures to curb money-laundering activities. It has participated in a number of international initiatives, including a Financial Action Task Force set up by the G-7 countries in 1989 to propose measures to combat money laundering. The task force has since issued a set of 40 recommendations for national and international action. Actions taken by Switzerland to combat money laundering have been based in large part on the recommendations of the Financial Action Task Force.[263]

The Swiss Criminal Code now makes it an offense for any one to commit an act the effect of which is to impede the identification of the source, discovery, or confiscation of assets that he knows, or should have known, came from a crime.[264] A crime under Swiss law includes most serious offenses, including theft, robbery, fraud, extortion, blackmail, kidnapping, and, of course, acceptance of bribes by public officials.[265] The offense is punishable in Switzerland, even if the underlying crime has been committed abroad, provided, of course, that the set of circumstances that constitute the underlying crime amounts to a crime under both Swiss law and the foreign law.[266]

The Swiss Criminal Code also makes it an offense for financial intermediaries to accept, keep on deposit, help to invest, or transfer assets of a third party without verifying the identity of the beneficial owner of such assets with the vigilance required by each particular set of circumstances.[267] After amendments introduced in March 1994, the code also provides for the right of persons to whom the relevant section applies to notify law enforcement authorities "of *indicia* founding a suspicion that the assets have a criminal origin."[268] The right to report this type of suspicion was the subject of legal controversy on account of the requirement of secrecy imposed by Swiss banking rules.[269]

The Money Laundering Act was enacted by Switzerland in October 1997. The purpose of the Act was to combat money laundering and ensure an adequate level of vigilance in financial transactions. The Act takes account of the outcome of several international initiatives taken to combat money laundering. It also supplements existing legislation, including the Swiss Criminal Code, in several ways.

First, the Money Laundering Act introduces a duty to report, according to which financial intermediaries are required to report the knowledge or suspicion of a criminal activity that they acquire in the course of their business relationship with their clients.[270] Attorneys and public notaries are exempt from the duty to report, but only to the extent that they acquire their knowledge or suspicion of a criminal activity in privileged circumstances.[271]

Second, in cases where a duty to report arises, the Act also imposes a duty on the financial intermediary to block the assets that are the subject matter of the report.[272] The purpose of this measure is obviously to avoid the disappearance of assets suspected to be the proceeds of a crime.[273] The blocking of assets is maintained for a period of no more than five business days, after which the funds are automatically released, unless in the meantime the competent law enforcement authorities have decided to intervene.[274]

Finally, the Act has a number of provisions designed to strengthen the implementation of the so-called "Know-Your-Customer" (KYC) rules and extend them to all financial intermediaries.[275] The KYC rules are an important element of the overall strategy to combat money laundering. They were part of the recommendations of the Financial Action Task Force, and include rules such as customer identification rules and bookkeeping rules, as well as an obligation to clarify the economic background of suspicious transactions.[276]

Latvia. The law on the Prevention of Proceeds Derived from Criminal Activity in Latvia was passed on December 18, 1997, and went into effect on June 1, 1998. According to an unofficial translation of the law, its purpose is to prevent the laundering of proceeds derived from criminal activities. To this effect, the law establishes the rights and responsibilities of financial institutions, credit institutions, and their supervisory and control activities, and it provides for the establishment of the Office for Preventing Laundering of Proceeds Derived from Criminal Activity (also referred to in the law as the Disclosures Office) and the Advisory Council.[277]

The Disclosures Office is described as an independent body, subject to the oversight authority of the Latvian Public Prosecutor's Office.[278] Its role is to receive, collect, store, and analyze reports made by credit and financial institutions, to determine whether there is sufficient evidence of money laundering and, if so, to assist law enforcement authorities and the courts to have the case heard and reach a final determination.[279] The Disclosures Office is also charged with responsibility to analyze information and provide guidance as appropriate to credit and financial institutions, and to cooperate with other state institutions. It does not, however, have any prosecutorial powers, nor does it appear to have any special powers of search and seizure or other enhanced investigative powers.

The purpose of the Advisory Council is to strengthen cooperation among state institutions for purposes of the law, advise on the list of indicators of unusual transactions, and make recommendations to the Disclosures Office on the performance of its functions under the law.[280] The Advisory Council consists of eight members, six of whom represent the private sector.[281]

For purposes of the definition of money laundering under the law, the activities that constitute criminal activities are described in some detail. They include "giving and taking of bribes, [and] intermediation in bribery."[282] They also include a host of other criminal activities ranging from smuggling and dealing in arms and ammunitions to organized crime, hostage taking, dealing in pornographic materials, and traffic in narcotic drugs.[283]

The law requires credit and financial institutions to refrain from conducting transactions that they suspect involve money laundering or attempted money laundering.[284] It sets forth the procedural measures to be followed by institutions to monitor financial transactions and report unusual or suspicious transactions and, thus, to avoid the possibility of the financial system being used for money-laundering purposes.[285] Transactions can be characterized as unusual or suspicious, according to a list of indicators of unusual transactions issued by the Disclosures Office that takes into account proposals of the Advisory Council, which have been approved by the Cabinet.[286] There are also provisions to protect credit and financial institutions in cases where they either pursue a transaction after duly reporting it to the Disclosures Office or refrain from pursuing the transaction altogether.[287]

Although the law appears to create an offense of money laundering, surprisingly, it does not precisely define the elements constituting such an offense. In particular, it does not make it clear whether, and to what extent, a conviction for the underlying criminal activity that forms the basis of the money-laundering activity is a precondition for a conviction on a money-laundering charge. It does not provide any guidance on the treatment of funds found or suspected to be the proceeds of a money-laundering offense. Although the law appears to suggest that the offense may be committed solely by credit and financial institutions, it is arguable that employees and customers may also be liable to commit specific offenses thereunder. Finally, the law does not provide for any specific penalties to deal with money-laundering offenses.

Offenses Involving Special Rules of Evidence

Many of the corruption offenses created under recently adopted corruption legislation involve the introduction of special rules of evidence, the effect of which is to ease the burden of proof resting on the prosecution and, in so doing, increase the odds of securing convictions. The introduction of new rules of evidence is not just a recognition of the sheer impossibility of establishing one or more of the elements of corruption charges; it also signals society's growing frustration with corruption, as well as its determination to develop appropriate legal techniques to arrest its pervasive influence. New rules of evidence have been introduced in relation to possession of unexplained wealth or property, bribery, and possession or control of property by close relatives or associates of accused parties.

Possession of Unexplained Wealth or Property. Hong Kong's Prevention of Bribery Act provides a classic example of policymakers' clear determination to ease the burden of proof resting on the prosecution and challenge some of the myths surrounding the constitutional rights of accused parties. In any proceedings against a public servant on account of the standard of living that he maintains or pecuniary resources or property under his control, it is for the accused, not the prosecution, to account satisfactorily for such standard of living or such pecuniary resources or property, as the case may be.[288] Even though the accused party bears the burden of proof on this one issue, the standard of proof that applies in the case of the accused is merely an evidential burden of adducing sufficient evidence to displace the legal presumption created by the Act, which operates in favor of the prosecution. Subject to the obligation of the accused to discharge the evidential burden in relation to one of the elements of the offense, the prosecution continues, in accordance with constitutional provisions governing the rights of accused parties, to bear the overall burden of establishing guilt.

Similarly, the Tanzanian Prevention of Corruption Act reverses the normal rules governing the onus of proof in a criminal case to the extent that it relieves the prosecution from having to establish one of the key elements of the offense—the element of corruptibility involved in the acquisition of property or in the receipt of benefit of services, as the case may be.[289] For a prima facie case to be established against the accused, it is enough for the prosecution to establish that the accused was a public officer; that, in that capacity, he or she acquired property or obtained the benefit of services; and that there are reasonable grounds to suspect that he or she corruptly acquired property or obtained the benefit of services, as the case may be. Provided a *prima facie* case has been made against the accused, the Act creates a legal presumption, the effect of which is to shift the burden of proof, requiring the accused to adduce sufficient evidence to show that he did not corruptly acquire property or receive the benefit of services; failing which, the property or the benefit of services is deemed to have been so acquired or so received, as the case may be.

There have been numerous attempts to challenge the constitutionality of provisions requiring an accused party to bear, at least in part, the burden of disproving guilt. Such provisions, it is argued, contravene the constitutionally guaranteed rights of accused parties and, in particular, the universally recognized presumption of innocence. Not surprisingly, such attempts have failed.[290] Corruption charges invariably involve a great deal of factual evidence, which lies within the exclusive knowledge of the accused party. To require the prosecution to establish elements of the charges that rely wholly or in part on such evidence would be to impose an impossible burden on the prosecution, which in turn would frustrate any attempt to secure convictions for corruption offenses. Ultimately, the constitutional issue that arises is whether it is reasonable to expect an accused party to adduce enough evidence of the source and origin of his wealth to rebut the presumption created by law, or whether such a requirement is so unbearable as to infringe the constitutional right to be presumed innocent until proven guilty. In an environment where practically every responsible government in the rest of the world has launched a worldwide campaign against corruption, it is unlikely that courts would invalidate a measure that might prove to be one of the ultimate tools in the combat against corruption, and one that can hardly amount to an undue imposition—except, precisely, in those cases in which accused parties have something to hide.

Bribery. One of the essential elements of the offense of bribery, according to Hong Kong's Prevention of Bribery Act, is that the advantage that is the subject matter of the bribery charge must have been given, offered, or accepted without lawful authority or reasonable excuse.[291] The Act provides that the burden of proving a defense of lawful authority or reasonable excuse lies with the accused.[292] Because the reversal of the onus of proof affects only one of the several elements that constitute the offense of bribery, the prosecution must prove all the other elements—namely, that a person has offered or given to a public servant, or a public servant has solicited or accepted, an advantage as an inducement or reward for any act or omission on the part of the public servant in the course of his official duties. It is only if the prosecution proves all these other elements of the offense, thereby establishing a *prima facie* case against the accused, that the reversed onus of proof provision comes into play, requiring the accused to establish a defense of lawful authority or reasonable excuse.

Similar provisions are found in both the Tanzanian Prevention of Corruption Act and Malawi Corrupt Practices Act. The Malawi Act provides that whenever it is proved in any proceedings under the Act that any person solicited, accepted, or obtained, or agreed to accept or attempted to receive or obtain, any payment in any of the circumstances set out in the relevant section under which the accused is charged, in the absence of evidence to the contrary, such payment shall be presumed to have been corruptly solicited, accepted, or obtained, or agreed to be accepted, received, or obtained.[293] The effect of this provision and the corresponding provision in the Tanzanian Prevention of Corruption Act[294] is to relieve the prosecution from having to establish the element of fraud involved in the offense—provided, of course, that all the other elements of the offense have been duly established and a *prima facie* case has been made out against the accused.

Reversing the burden of proof in criminal cases is a serious matter, which no legislature is likely to take lightly. It is also a reflection of the seriousness with which society perceives corruption, as well as its growing frustration with the magnitude of the task facing corruption law enforcement agencies. Whether or not it amounts to an infringement of the right of the accused to be presumed innocent until proven guilty is a question that must be addressed on a case–by-case basis. Courts are bound to take a dim view of any attempt to use this device to shift onto the accused the substantive burden of disproving essential elements of the offense. In Hong Kong, however, as in Malawi and Tanzania, not every innocent act triggers a reversal of the burden of proof in a bribery case. In Hong Kong, a shift in the burden of proof does not come into play unless and until the prosecution establishes both the existence of a transaction between a public servant and another person involving an advantage accruing to the public servant, and a direct relationship between the advantage and an act or omission on the part of the public servant in the exercise of his official functions. Reversing the burden of proof in such circumstances, with regard to a possible defense or attenuating circumstances that are within the exclusive knowledge of the accused, can hardly be regarded as an imposition: It is a small price to pay to promote the chances of victory against the organized forces of corruption.

Possession or Control of Property by Close Relatives or Associates. Section 9(2) of the Tanzanian Prevention of Corruption Act creates an additional presumption with respect to property alleged to have been corruptly acquired or the benefit of services alleged to have been corruptly received by an accused party. In cases where such property is found to have been acquired or the benefit of services found to have been received by a person other than the accused party, the court may, in appropriate cases, having regard to that other person's relationship with the accused, infer that such property was acquired or such benefit of services received by that other person on behalf of the accused. In such cases, the prosecution is relieved from having to establish one of the elements of the offense— namely, that it was the accused himself who acquired property or received the benefit of services.

A similar legal presumption is found in the Malawi Corrupt Practices Act, the effect of which is to relieve the prosecution from having to establish actual possession or control of pecuniary resources or other property by an accused party, in cases where such pecuniary resources or other property is held by another person, and a court of law is satisfied, because of that other person's close relationship to the accused or other circumstances, that such pecuniary resources or other property is held in trust on behalf of an accused, or has been acquired as a gift or loan without adequate consideration from the latter.[295] A similar provision is to be found in the Hong Kong Prevention of Bribery Act.[296]

The presumption relating to property in the possession or control of close friends and associates of accused parties in corruption cases is another indispensable tool in the fight against corruption. It is an attempt to preempt a commonly used technique in corruption cases to divert the illegal proceeds of corruption and disguise their source and origin. Without it, many corrupt transactions would remain immune to scrutiny, and their perpetrators would go unpunished. The basis for the presumption is the recognition that much of the factual evidence relating to transfers of property between an accused party and his close relatives or associates is within their own exclusive knowledge. To require the prosecution to adduce evidence of such dealings would be to place an impossible burden on the prosecution of corruption charges.

Like other legal presumptions, this presumption is open to challenge on the grounds that it may cause otherwise innocent transactions to be subjected to legal scrutiny, solely because of the relationship between the accused party and the person in possession or control of property. Notwithstanding the potential for abuse that every such legal presumption entails, it is arguable, on the basis of the relevant provisions of the corruption laws of Hong Kong, Malawi, and Tanzania, that the presumption does not apply except in cases where the prosecution has established that suspicious circumstances surround the source or origin of the property, and then only to the extent that it is not subsequently disproved by evidence to the contrary to be adduced by those who are the most likely repositories of such evidence.

Sanctions and Penalties

It has been said of the anticorruption laws that, for all their elaborate provisions, they have failed to deter corruption or have any measurable impact on its level and prevalence. Anticorruption laws have been on the statute books for centuries and, in many cases, continue to co-exist alongside new corruption laws. The advent of new anticorruption legislation, it is argued, has not been accompanied by any renewed effort to root out corruption and expose corrupt practices. It has merely provided many policymakers with badly needed breathing time as they come under pressure to repudiate corrupt practices and join in worldwide efforts to combat corruption. Adoption of new corruption-related laws has provided the political leadership in many countries with a unique opportunity to provide a solid display of their commitment to fight corruption, without any concomitant need for immediate follow-up action to enforce such laws.

Adoption of laws is not an end in itself, and, in the final analysis, it is for each country to use its new laws to demonstrate its willingness to fight corruption. Laws alone are of limited value in any anticorruption strategy if they are not also supported by the requisite measure of political will, as well as appropriate institutions and mechanisms to enforce them. From a purely technical point of view, however, the new anticorruption laws have enhanced the ability of countries to combat corruption in at least four respects.

First, as a rule, new corruption-related laws provide for much stiffer sentences and harsher penalties than were available under traditional corruption legislation. The penalty provided for corruption offenses under Malawi's Corrupt Practices Act ranges from 5 to 12 years' imprisonment.[297] Corresponding offenses under the Tanzania's Prevention of Corruption Act are punishable with imprisonment of up to 14 years and a fine.[298] The penalty for bribery and related offenses under Hong Kong's Prevention of

Bribery Act is imprisonment of up to 10 years and a fine, which may include the amount or value of any advantage received or, in case of a conviction for an offense of possession of pecuniary resources or property that has not been satisfactorily accounted for, the value of the pecuniary resources or property.[299]

Second, in addition to other penalties provided under the new anticorruption laws, there are also provisions for the attachment and forfeiture of property that is the proceeds of corruption offenses. Provisions for the attachment of property[300] that is the subject matter of corruption charges and, upon a conviction, for its forfeiture,[301] are to be found in Tanzania's Prevention of Corruption Act. Under Hong Kong's Prevention of Bribery Act, where any person is suspected of, or charged with, an offense, the court may issue a restraining order in respect of any property in that person's possession or under his control, or in the possession or under the control of any other person acting for, or on behalf of, the person so suspected of, or charged with, an offense. The effect of the restraining order is to restrict the right of any person to whom the order is addressed to dispose of or otherwise deal with the property except in accordance with the terms of the order.[302] Upon a conviction for possession of pecuniary resources or other property that has not been satisfactorily accounted for under the Act, other provisions enable the court to order the confiscation of pecuniary resources or other property not exceeding pecuniary resources or other property that is the subject matter of the conviction.[303]

Third, the new laws have introduced a number of legal presumptions that have significantly eased the burden of proof that normally rests on the prosecution with respect to specific elements of the charges in criminal cases in general. One such legal presumption relieves the prosecution from having to establish the element of fraud in bribery cases, provided, of course, that all the other elements of the offense have been established. Another relieves the prosecution from having to prove that property is in the possession of an accused party or under his control, if such property is in the possession or under the control of a close friend or associate of the accused, and the court is satisfied, having regard to that person's relationship to the accused or other circumstances, that such property is held on trust on behalf of the accused party or was received as a gift or loan and without sufficient consideration from the latter. A third presumption applies in cases of possession of unexplained pecuniary resources or property, requiring an accused party charged with such an offense to give a satisfactory account of his pecuniary resources or property, failing which the court is entitled to assume that the accused has none and proceed to convict him accordingly. The introduction of legal presumptions relieves the prosecution from having to adduce factual evidence that is largely, if not exclusively, within the knowledge of accused parties without necessarily infringing the rights of the accused to be presumed innocent until proven guilty.

Finally, the introduction of money-laundering legislation has added a new dimension to the anticorruption movement. Money laundering is to bribery and other economic crimes what possession of stolen property is to theft. It tracks down the proceeds of economic crimes in the hands of third parties, thereby providing alternative charges for indictments based not so much on the conduct of the original perpetrators of the bribery or other economic crimes as on the tainted origin of the proceeds of the crimes. Although it is not uncommon to charge one and the same person with both money laundering and the economic crime on which the money laundering charge is based, it is more common to rely on money-laundering legislation to proceed against those who seek to obscure or disguise the proceeds of economic crimes, thereby aiding and abetting the perpetrators of such crimes. Money-laundering legislation has had the effect of considerably expanding the nexus of parties liable to be called to account as a result of any single economic crime. Its objective is to make sure that any subsequent transaction involving the proceeds of a corruption or other economic crime shall not, in and of itself, have the effect of relieving such proceeds of their tainted origin.

Corruption Redefined

A review of anticorruption legislation in force in different parts of the world reveals striking similarities, as well as basic differences, in the approach followed from one country to another. The similarities are obvious. First and foremost, they are to be found in the basic elements that constitute the offense of corruption. In substance, as this study has illustrated, these elements vary little from one country to another. Anticorruption legislation in most newly developed and developing countries has been largely based on the existing laws of other, more developed countries, which have been used as models to be built upon and adapted, as needed, to local circumstances. In so doing, most major legal systems appear to have settled on a fairly standard basic definition of corruption, treating it as consummated whenever a public officer or other agent accepts or solicits a bribe, or any person gives or promises a bribe to such a public officer or other agent; provided, however, that the purpose of the bribe is to serve as a reward to the public officer or agent for an act that he has done or refrained from doing in the exercise of his functions, or as an inducement designed to ensure that the public officer or agent does, or refrains from doing, any act, in the exercise of his functions.

Although there is consensus on the core definition of corruption, there are also other aspects of the definition that have been subject to controversy. Several of these aspects merit further attention. They are, first, the definition of a bribe; second, the relevance of the value of the bribe, whether small or large, insignificant, or of a routine nature, and the related issue of local customs; third, the relative importance of public and private corruption; and, finally, the effect of the consent of a principal to an act of corruption committed by an agent or public officer.

Definition of a Bribe. The definition of what constitutes a bribe has varied from one jurisdiction to another. In the United Kingdom, as in Kenya, a bribe is defined as a gift, loan, fee, reward, or advantage. The term "advantage," however, is subject to an even more elaborate definition, including "any office, dignity, or any forbearance to demand any money or money's worth or valuable thing, . . . any aid, vote, consent or influence, . . . or the holding out of any expectation of any gift, loan, fee, reward, or advantage . . . ."[304]

In Tanzania, the central element of the corruption offense is an advantage, which is defined as a gift of any property, movable or immovable; loan, fee, or reward, including valuable consideration of any kind; discount; commission; rebate; bonus; deduction or percentage; employment or services; or an agreement to give employment or render services.[305] A similar definition is to be found in the Corrupt Practices Act of Malawi.[306] In U.S. bribery legislation, a bribe is referred to as "anything of value."[307] In a recent policy study on corruption,[308] the World Bank has also injected its own definition of corruption: abuse of public office for private gain.

As the scope and extent of corruption have expanded in recent years, some of the limitations inherent in the traditional definition of a bribe have gradually come to light. Although bribery has for a long time been associated with the concept of a tangible gift, loan, or reward, the classic definition of a bribe has evolved over the years to cover less tangible benefits, such as any aid, vote, consent, or influence or employment or services, or an agreement to give employment or render services. This evolution notwithstanding, there has been little attempt to do away with the tangible or pecuniary element that has mainly characterized the crime of bribery in many jurisdictions. The World Bank's own definition of corruption is a case in point.

The emphasis on the tangible and pecuniary elements of bribery has tended to obscure the role that other less tangible benefits or advantages can play in corruption cases. Examples of such intangible benefits and advantages that drive corruption include cronyism, patronage, and nepotism, which are correctly identified as potential sources of corruption in the recent World Bank policy study on corruption.[309] There are jurisdictions in which the offense of corruption is so defined as to allow for prosecution of bribery cases, irrespective of whether the bribes are of the tangible pecuniary variety or not. In many other instances, however, this is not the case. A candidate for public office or a bidder for a contract who offers sexual favors to a public official in order to attain his objective is no less guilty of corruption than one who offers money or other pecuniary advantages to achieve the same purpose. Similarly, a political leader who holds out a promise of access to the party leadership, whether express or implied, or the mere prospect of future benevolence, to procure employment or other contracts on behalf of friends and relatives should not escape punishment solely on account of the fact that the benefits in question are not quantifiable. As cronyism, patronage, and nepotism continue to take their toll on the social and economic progress of many countries, it may perhaps be time to recognize that they are as much a source of corruption as bribery and ought to be dealt with accordingly.

Insignificance or Routine Nature of a Bribe. The small value of a bribe, its insignificance and routine nature, and reliance on local customs have all been cited in one form or another as possible defenses to a charge of bribery. The existence of such defenses based on value or customs has been reaffirmed from time to time in some countries and, needless to say, challenged in others. Having regard to the diversity of circumstances that prevail from one country to another, it is not likely that there will ever be any consensus on the validity of such defenses.

In Malawi, the definition of the gratification that is the core element of the corruption offense has been adjusted to exclude a casual gift, which has been defined as "any conventional hospitality on a modest scale or an unsolicited gift of modest value not exceeding K500 offered to a person in recognition or appreciation of his services, or as a gesture of goodwill towards him, and includes any inexpensive seasonal gift offered to staff or associates by public and private bodies or private individuals on festive or other special occasions, which is not in any way connected with the performance of a person's official duty . . . ."[310] Under the U.S. Foreign Corrupt Practices Act, a similar exception is provided for payments to foreign officials, political parties, or party officials for the purpose of expediting or securing the performance of so-called routine governmental actions.[311] Conversely, in Hong Kong, it is expressly provided that it is not a defense to show that the advantage that is the subject matter of a bribery offense is customary in any profession, trade, vocation, or calling.[312]

In actual practice, regardless of the existence or otherwise of a defense based on local custom or the value of the bribe, it is uncommon in most jurisdictions for charges to be brought for bribery based solely on an allegation pertaining to a small or insignificant bribe, or one generally regarded as consistent with normal practice or local custom. Even if such charges are brought and established, the penalty is unlikely to be more than a symbolic one. Whether or not what is regarded as ordinary practice can be regarded as corrupt is one of the issues with which the U.K. Law Commission was confronted in its recent review of corruption legislation. A common example of ordinary practice that the Law Commission had in mind was that of corporate hospitality. What prevents an ordinary practice from being corrupt, the commission concluded, is not so much that it is ordinary, but that in general it creates no substantial conflict of interest between the recipients' interests and their duty.[313] The Law Commission's conclusion would be hard to challenge. Although the commission reached this conclusion in relation to "normal practice" corruption, the same principle is equally applicable in respect of small value or insignificant bribes.

Public versus Private Corruption. It comes as no surprise that corruption in the public sector has attracted more attention than corruption in the private sector. As the U.K. Law Commission has pointed out in its recent report on corruption legislation, the public expects higher standards of behavior from those in public life, occupying offices of public responsibility, or paid by the state than it expects from those who work for private companies.[314] That is not to suggest that corruption is more widespread or pervasive in the public sector than in the private sector. Although public sector corruption has often generated more publicity than private sector corruption, there is growing concern about corruption in the private sector.

In the United Kingdom, the Public Bodies Corrupt Practices Act was passed in 1889. As its name implies, it was concerned solely with bribery in the public sector. It was not until 1906 that the Prevention of Corruption Act was passed. The 1906 Act was intended to apply to all agents, whether in the public or private sector. Modern corruption legislation in Hong Kong, Tanzania, and Malawi apply equally to private and public sector corruption. However, the World Bank's study on corruption restricts its concern for and definition of corruption to its incidence in the public sector. Although the Bank recognizes that bribery exists in the private sector, the study explains that "bribery in the public sector, offered or extracted, should be the Bank's main concern, since the Bank lends primarily to governments and supports government policies, programs, and projects."[315]

It has long been assumed that corruption in the public sector is more damaging to the public interest, and therefore a more serious offense, than corruption in the private sector. But, as the U.K. Law Commission has pointed out, this assumption has become increasingly suspect.[316] There are at least three reasons that account for the growing interest in corruption in the private sector. First, to suggest that corruption in the private sector is less serious than corruption in the public sector is to create a double standard that is hard to justify on moral, ethical, or economic grounds, and, in so doing, send the wrong signals on the moral standards expected of the private sector.

Second, as more and more public sector functions are being privatized or taken over by the private sector, the line between the public and private sectors has become increasingly difficult to draw. Where public utility entities have been privatized, as has been the case in many countries, there is no apparent reason why corruption in that sector ought to be treated less harshly solely because that sector has been privatized.

Finally, it is questionable whether corruption in the private sector is less damaging to the public interest than in the public sector. Large-scale corruption in the private sector results in higher consumer prices and reduced tax revenues, bringing about significant losses in earnings and revenue shortfalls, as it does in the public sector.

Consent of Principal. The offense of bribery as commonly defined presupposes the existence of a duty of trust between the agent and the agent's principal. The breach of that duty by the agent forms the basis of the offense. Regardless of whether the breach of duty originates with the agent or is instigated by a third party, there is no offense, according to this hypothesis, unless the principal's trust has been betrayed.[317]

Based on this hypothesis, there has been some speculation that the consent of the principal is an effective defense to a charge of bribery. There is no breach of trust, it is argued, if the principal consents to the alleged act of bribery. Others have argued that the consent of the principal can be a defense, but only in cases that do not involve a breach of a public duty. This distinction between the private sector and the public sector assumes— somewhat optimistically—that the principal's consent or lack thereof is more easily ascertainable in a private sector context than in the public sector.

The better view, it is submitted, is that the consent of the principal is a sufficient defense in both the private and public sector contexts, provided, of course, that such consent can be appropriately verified. Of course, such consent will be more easily ascertained in cases of a principal who happens to be a single individual than in the context of the public sector or a large corporation. A waiter who adjusts the quality of the service provided according to the size of his tip is not guilty of soliciting bribery: The practice of taking tips is consistent with normal practice, and it is a practice that is accepted, if not actively encouraged, by his employer. Assuming that similar practices were ever to be extended to the public sector or even large corporations, they would presumably, depending on the power structure involved, require prior legislative or board of directors' approval, as the case may be.

IV
International Efforts Against Corruption

No universally applicable law pertaining to the combat against corruption has been adopted to date. However, there have been numerous regional and international efforts to assist in the reduction and possible eradication of corruption. These efforts started in the early 1970s, when there was significant interest in the increasing role of multinational corporations in the world economy. They have continued over the years, and the 1990s have engendered much interest in this subject.

U.N. Efforts

U.N. Initiatives in the 1970s

In 1974, the Economic and Social Council of the United Nations (ECOSOC) established an intergovernmental subsidiary body, the Commission on Transnational Corporations (CTC), with the objective of furthering a better understanding of the nature of transnational corporations and their political, legal, and economic effects on host and home countries. Another objective was to secure effective international arrangements aimed at enhancing the contribution of such corporations to national development goals and world economic growth, while controlling and eliminating their negative effects. The main aim of the CTC was to prepare for adoption by the United Nations a Code of Conduct on Transnational Corporations, which would offer credible assurances to both host countries and home countries in the treatment of various issues, such as tax and foreign exchange requirements, and in the stability, confidence, and transparency required in international transactions. The CTC also dealt with one of the negative aspects of such transactions—the problem of corrupt practices.

This exercise was to be carried out by the Ad Hoc Intergovernmental Working Group on the Problem of Corrupt Practices, established in August 1976, and ECOSOC, after General Assembly Resolution 3514 (XXXXX) of December 15, 1975. Its outcome was due to be reflected in an article in the proposed code of conduct. This resolution expressed concern over corrupt practices in the activities of certain transnational corporations and requested ECOSOC to include this question in the work of the CTC. The Ad Hoc Intergovernmental Working Group worked with the CTC to produce several drafts on the issue of bribery and corruption and, in particular, a draft of an international agreement on illicit payments.[318] The Ad Hoc Working Group was replaced by the Committee on an International Agreement on Illicit Payments, which was established by ECOSOC on August 4, 1978.[319]

After 12 meetings, the committee agreed on a draft text of an international agreement that was transmitted to ECOSOC and the CTC for inclusion in the relevant article the code of conduct which was under preparation. The principal corruption-related provision in this agreement required each contracting state to make punishable by appropriate criminal penalties under its law several specified acts. These include:

(a) The offering, promising or giving of any payment, gift or other advantage by any natural person, on his own behalf or on behalf of any enterprise or any other person whether juridical or natural, to or for the benefit of a public official as undue consideration for performing or refraining from the performance of his duties in 22connection with an international commercial transaction.

(b) The soliciting, demanding, accepting or receiving, directly or indirectly, by a public official of any payment, gift or other advantage, as undue consideration for performing or refraining from the performance of his duties pertaining to an international commercial transaction.

The term "public official" was defined broadly to include both appointed or elected officials at the national, regional, or local level who are employees of a government or public or governmental authority or who perform a public function. Other interesting features in this draft agreement related to cooperation between states in connection with criminal investigations and prosecutions in respect of offenses covered by the agreement and the fact that any such offenses are "deemed to be included as extraditable offenses in any extradition treaty existing between Contracting States."[320] After this significant foray into this problem area, the draft agreement was never adopted and put into operation by ECOSOC. However, some of the principles underlying this work have found their way into the more recent initiatives discussed in the following sections.

The U.N. Declaration against Corruption and Bribery

The United Nations' confirmed interest in the subject of corruption over the last two decades (after the earlier discussions on illicit payments) culminated on December 16, 1996, with the adoption by the General Assembly of a Declaration against Corruption and Bribery.[321] As part of this resolution, the General Assembly also adopted an International Code of Conduct for Public Officials.

Despite its nonbinding nature, this declaration comprehensively covers the issues. It broadly defines bribery to include all actions deemed to be included in the laws on bribery and corruption in many states.[322] It urges states to take necessary action for the adoption of laws to combat these practices, including the development or maintenance of accounting standards and practices, as well as appropriate business codes and best practices. In this connection, it recommends that states take action not only to deny the tax deductibility of bribes paid by enterprises in such states to elected or public officials of another state, but also to make illicit enrichment by public officials and elected representatives an offense. Its most far-reaching recommendations concern cooperation among states. It provides that states should afford each other the greatest possible assistance in connection with criminal investigations and legal proceedings brought in respect of corruption and bribery in international commercial transactions. This cooperation includes, without limitation, the production of documents and other information and facilitation of access to documentation about transactions and about the identity of persons engaged in bribery, notice to other states about the initiation of criminal proceedings and their outcomes, and more liberal application of extradition laws.

Regional Efforts

The concern and discussion about corruption continued unabated at the national level and also in a significant number of international forums in the 1980s. Every major corruption-related scandal in both developed and developing countries elicited international condemnation as well as calls for more significant action by both multinational corporations and states. The 1990s have, however, seen concerted action on the part of regional groups, as well as within the framework of multilateral organizations. This interest has in part been fueled by the notion of "good governance," another issue of major concern in the 1990s.

Efforts within the Organization of American States: Inter-American Convention against Corruption

One of the landmark expressions of concern and possible action on the issue of corruption was taken by member nations of the Organization of

American States (OAS) in 1996. The Inter-American Convention against Corruption was signed by 21 Latin American countries in March 1996 and by the United States and Canada later the same year. [323] It entered into force on March 20, 1997, with the deposit of instruments of ratification by Paraguay and Bolivia. Several other countries have since ratified the convention, which was signed after more than two years of negotiations.

The main objective of the convention is to promote the development and strengthening of legal mechanisms in signatory countries to "prevent, detect, punish and eradicate"[324] official corruption in both the domestic and international spheres. It is a major treaty in terms of both its form and substance. Its main focus is, however, to require contracting parties to criminalize bribery of both local and foreign officials and also to enact measures to combat the illicit enrichment of public officials. The convention defines corruption very broadly to include "solicitation or acceptance of a bribe, offering or granting of a bribe, inappropriate acts or omissions of public officials (includes government officials), fraudulent use or concealment of property derived from any such action and participation, collaboration or conspiracy to commit any of such acts."[325] Even though states agree to take all necessary actions to promulgate laws to prohibit or punish persons allegedly violating the laws on corruption, the convention includes a provision that appears to potentially limit the obligation of contracting states. It provides that a state's obligations under the convention are "subject to its Constitution and the fundamental principles of its legal system.".[326]

The convention introduced interesting provisions that follow up on the discussions in the 1970s on unjust or illicit enrichment of public officials and are reminiscent of the more recent anticorruption laws in Malawi and Tanzania. Article IX requires the parties to the convention to establish a new offense of illicit enrichment where there is "a significant increase in the assets of a government official that he/she cannot reasonably explain in relation to his/her lawful earnings during the performance of his/her functions." It is interesting to note that where a state does not criminalize such enrichment, such state is required, insofar as its laws permit, to cooperate with other states that are parties to the convention in the enforcement of the other states' laws. In addition, the convention takes an expansive view of the notion of corruption by making certain acts that have not normally been considered "corrupt practices" to be so considered. These include "(i) the improper use of classified or confidential information obtained by a public official for his own benefit or that of a third party; (ii) the improper use of property belonging to a state by a public official for the same purposes, (iii) any attempt by a person to obtain a decision from a public authority whereby he/she illicitly obtains for himself/herself illicit benefits, and (iv) cases where movable or immovable properties are diverted by a public official for his own benefit or that of a third party."[327] If the areas identified are criminalized as required by the convention, such laws potentially will have the effect of closing some of the remaining loopholes in this area.

The convention also deals with the issue of governance in general and requires states to take measures to ensure good governance, such as those related to transparency and accountability in governmental activities. The rules and procedures concerning procurement are also given some prominence, as is the adoption of codes to promote ethical behavior by public officials.[328] The question of the tax treatment for expenditures made in violation of the anticorruption laws of other states is also dealt with by the convention.[329]

Efforts within the Organisation for Economic Co-operation and Development (OECD)

The OECD Recommendations. A noteworthy international instrument outlining a program of action for the combat against bribery and corruption in international business transactions is to be found in the final OECD Council Recommendations on Combating Bribery in International Business Transactions, adopted on May 23, 1997.[330]

Apart from generally recognizing the fact that bribery is a widespread phenomenon in international business transactions, the OECD Council Recommendations note that corruption raises serious moral and political concerns and distorts international competition in business transactions. These consequences are also fully recognized in the various U.N. instruments and those from other forums. The OECD instrument recommends that expenditures originating from bribery of public officials should not be granted tax deductibility in countries and stresses the importance of the assurance of transparency through the maintenance of proper accounts, establishment of appropriate controls, and auditing.[331] However, its most important contribution to the efforts aimed at alleviating the concerns about bribery and corruption is its distillation of common elements of criminal legislation.[332]

According to the recommendations, the first element of bribery is the promise or giving of any undue payment or other advantages, whether directly or through intermediaries, to a public official, for him- or herself or for a third party, to influence the official to act or to refrain from acting in the performance of his or her official duties to obtain or retain business. The second element is that the term "foreign public official" includes any person holding a legislative, administrative, or judicial office of a foreign country or in an international organization, whether appointed or elected, or any person exercising a public function or task in a foreign country. A third element is the offeror, who can be any person who makes an offer or gives a bribe, or on whose behalf an offer is made or a bribe given. An ancillary element is that the general criminal law concepts of attempt, complicity, and conspiracy of the law of the prosecuting state should be recognized as applicable to the offense of bribery of a foreign public official. Hence, bribery of foreign public officials to obtain or retain business is an offense irrespective of the value or outcome of the bribe, perceptions of local custom, or tolerance of bribery by local authorities.[333]

Another important element dealt with in the OECD Council Recommendations relates to the issue of jurisdiction. Jurisdiction over the offense of bribery of foreign public officials should be established when the offense is committed in whole or in part in the prosecuting state's territory. The territorial basis for jurisdiction should be interpreted broadly so that an extensive physical connection to the act of bribery is not required. Moreover, states that prosecute their nationals for offenses committed abroad should do so in respect of the bribery of foreign public officials according to the same principles. In contrast, states that do not prosecute on the basis of the nationality principle should be prepared to extradite their nationals when they are accused of bribery of foreign public officials.[334]

The recommendations further provide that the offense of bribery of foreign public officials should be sanctioned and punishable by effective, proportionate, and dissuasive criminal penalties, sufficient to secure effective mutual legal assistance and extradition, comparable with those applicable to the bribers in cases of corruption of domestic public officials. Monetary or other civil, administrative, or criminal penalties on any legal person involved should be provided, taking into account the amount of the bribe and the profits derived from the transaction obtained through the bribe. Forfeiture or confiscation of instrumentalities and of the benefits of the bribe and the profits derived from the transaction obtained through the bribe should be provided for, or comparable fines or damages imposed.[335]

Efficient enforcement is another element promoted by the recommendations. In view of the seriousness of the offense of bribery of foreign public officials, public prosecutors should exercise their discretion independently, based on professional motives. They should not be influenced by national economic interests, fostering good political relations, or the identity of the victim. Victims' complaints should be seriously investigated by the competent authorities. The statute of limitations should allow adequate time to address this complex offense, and states should provide adequate resources to prosecuting authorities so as to permit effective prosecution of bribery of foreign public officials.

OECD Council Recommendations provide a good framework for the development of the elements, both procedural and otherwise, of the crimes of bribery and corruption. These recommendations were further supplemented by the 1997 OECD Convention on Combating Bribery of Foreign Public Officials in International Business Transactions.

The OECD Convention on Combating Bribery of Foreign Public Officials in International Business Transactions. The issue of corruption has also been included periodically in the discussions among the G-7 heads of state. This subject was more specifically discussed as an agenda item during the meeting of the G-7 heads of state in Lyon, France, in 1996. After a reportedly lively debate, the conclusions of the discussions were included in the communiqué as follows:

> We are resolved to combat corruption in international business transactions, which is detrimental to transparency and fairness and imposes heavy economic and political costs. In keeping with the commitment of OECD Ministers to criminalize such bribery in an effective and coordinated manner, we urge the OECD to further examine the modalities and appropriate international instruments to facilitate criminalization and consider proposals for action in 1997.[336]

It is not surprising that the OECD was also discussing the issue of corruption at the same time that the United Nations, World Bank, International Monetary Fund, OAS, Council of Europe, and European Union were all working to advance international understanding of ways to combat corruption. After calling on OECD countries to criminalize foreign bribery, eliminate the tax deductibility of bribes to foreign public officials, and develop guidelines to be used in drafting legislation for the combat of bribery and corruption, the OECD Council of Ministers finally, on November 21, 1997, adopted the Convention on Combating Bribery of Foreign Public Officials in International Business Transactions.[337] The convention focuses on the criminalization of the bribery of foreign public officials. There had been considerable discussion since 1977 of how member countries of the OECD could match the provisions of the U.S. Foreign Corrupt Practices Act.

Parties to the OECD convention are required to take all measures necessary to establish the crime of bribery of a foreign public official.[338] The term "foreign public official" is defined broadly to include most public officials, including officials of parastatal entities and agents or officials of public international organizations, but the definition excludes officials of political parties or candidates for public office.[339] According to the Commentaries on the Convention, it is an offense to bribe or obtain or retain business or other improper advantage whether or not the briber concerned was the qualified bidder or could properly have been awarded the business. It is also noteworthy that small facilitation payments are not intended to be covered by Article 1 and are therefore not punishable.

The convention provides that the crime of bribery of a foreign public official should be punishable by effective, proportionate, and dissuasive criminal penalties. Further, the range of penalties should be comparable with that applicable to bribery in the case of the state party's own public officials, which may include imprisonment.[340] Another interesting provision is the relationship between this crime and money laundering. The convention provides that the crime of bribery of a foreign public official should be made a predicate offense for money-laundering legislation if a party to the convention has made either active or passive bribery of its own public officials such an offense.[341] Finally, the parties are required to cooperate in carrying out a program of systematic follow-up to monitor and promote the full implementation of the convention.[342] Follow-up of implementation will be done within the purview of the work of the OECD Working Group on Bribery in International Business Transactions.[343]

Efforts within The Council of Europe: The Criminal Law Convention

Review of international instruments dealing with the combat against corruption would not be complete without acknowledgment of the contribution of the Council of Europe. At their 19th Conference held in Valletta, Malta, in 1994, the European Ministers of Justice considered that corruption was a serious threat to democracy, the rule of law, and human rights. The Council of Europe then called upon its membership to respond to that threat. The ministers were convinced that it was necessary to adopt appropriate legislation in this area, and that a multidisciplinary approach was needed. They recommended the creation of a multidisciplinary group under the aegis of the European Committee on Crime Problems (CDPC) and the European Committee on Legal Cooperation (CDCJ), to be vested with the responsibility of examining the possibility of drafting model laws or codes of conduct, including international conventions on the subject.

In light of these recommendations, in September 1994, the ministers' committee established a Multidisciplinary Group on Corruption (MGC) and requested the MGC to examine suitable measures to be included in an international program of action against corruption. The MGC was also asked to make proposals to the Committee of Ministers before the end of 1995 as to the priorities and working structures, taking due account of the work of other international organizations. The MGC prepared a draft program of action against corruption, which was endorsed in January 1996 by the Committee of Ministers, who in turn invited the CDPC and the CDCJ to express their opinions. In the meantime, the Committee of Ministers further requested the MGC to begin the implementation of some of the actions in the program, such as work on one or more international instruments.[344]

The Committee of Ministers formally adopted a Program of Action in November 1996 and instructed the MGC to implement it before the end of the year 2000. In accordance with the objectives of the Program of Action and on the basis of interim terms of reference, the Criminal Law Working Group of the MGC (MGCP) began work on a draft criminal law convention in 1996. Between February 1996 and November 1997, the MGCP held 10 meetings and completed two full readings of the draft convention. In November 1997, they sent the text to the MGC for consideration. After several internal meetings and consultation within the MGC, the CDPC approved the draft convention in September 1998 and submitted it to the Committee of Ministers, which formally adopted the convention and decided to open it for signature.

The Criminal Law Convention, which was opened for signature on December 1, 1998, principally aims at developing common standards concerning certain corruption offenses. The convention reflects the Council of Europe's comprehensive approach to the fight against corruption. It provides a detailed, although not uniform, definition of activities covered by the term "corruption." These include both active and passive bribery, as well as trading in influence over the decisionmaking of public officials and money laundering. In scope, the convention is not limited to public officials. It covers, among others, private parties, foreign entities, senior officials of international organizations, elected representatives of international bodies, and judges and officials of international courts. In addition to the substantive as well as procedural law matters relevant to corruption offenses, the convention also seeks to improve international cooperation.[345] It provides for cooperation and assistance among the parties in the investigation of corrupt acts and the confiscation of proceeds emanating from such acts, as well as additional remedies for their victims.

The African Initiative

The issue of corruption has been a subject that has found great interest in Africa. It has been one of the facets of many of the discussions on governance issues in countries and in African regional forums, including the Organization of African Unity and various subregional institutions, such as the Economic Community of West African States. The problem of corruption and its threat to the development prospects of African countries has been a topical issue during deliberations in plenary sessions of the Global Coalition for Africa (GCA), a coalition of senior governmental officials from Africa and OECD countries, who meet periodically to discuss development issues of relevance to Africa and provide a voice and support for African development-related issues on the world scene. This issue was considered to be one that needed urgent attention at the meeting of the GCA Plenary in Maastricht, the Netherlands, in November 1995, prompting the GCA Co-chairpersons to decide that corruption and development should be a main topic of one of their annual policy forums. Thus, corruption was the main issue of discussion at the GCA Forum in Maputo, Mozambique, in November 1997. This forum was attended by several heads of state from Africa, as well as senior government officials from both Africa and OECD countries and representatives of international organizations such as the World Bank.

Discussions at this meeting were based on a study prepared by the GCA Secretariat, which contained recommendations for combating corruption, primarily at the national level but also at the international level in connection with international business transactions. It noted that preventing corruption required a consistent, coherent, broad-based approach and a long-term perspective. The proposed framework emphasized the importance of leadership and political will, reform of the public sector and the implementation of broad policy reform aimed at reducing government involvement in their economies (that is, the promotion of the private sector), streamlining government functions, limiting the discretionary decisionmaking authority of officials, and strengthening the judicial, executive, and legislative branches of governments. It was also considered important to create autonomous and independent watchdog agencies and to significantly increase the role of civil society.[346] On the international front, the study focuses on the increased role that international institutions, including the World Bank, United Nations Development Programme, and African Development Bank, should continue to play in the improvement of governance in African countries as well as efforts within such institutions to limit the opportunities for rent seeking and corrupt practices in their programs of assistance.[347]

The meeting was a resounding success. Several of the presidents and prime ministers confronted the issues in public for the first time, and the common elements of anticorruption programs were generally agreed to by all concerned. At the national level, these elements included direct and forceful support of the highest political leadership for the improvement of mechanisms to ensure transparency and accountability, introduction of independent watchdog bodies, reduction and simplification of government regulations, and improving procurement procedures.[348] At the international level, the forum urged the criminalization of bribery in international business transactions and the end of tax deductibility of bribes, as well as support by the international community to African countries to assist them to build capacity and establish effective systems to combat corrupt practices.[349]

Since this meeting, discussions on this issue have continued in Africa and elsewhere. A representative group of African, European and North American countries, and international organizations, such as the OECD and the World Bank, are collaborating to develop an appropriate framework to address the issue of corruption. On October 8, 1998, a preliminary meeting was held under the auspices of the GCA and the U.S. government. Various issues were discussed, including the strengthening of regional and international cooperation to address corruption and, in particular, how existing regional cooperation can be further strengthened and formalized. Possible areas of action were suggested, including consideration of anticorruption charters or conventions, development of regional networks and mechanisms to exchange information, training programs to strengthen police capacity and encourage cross-border police cooperation, and the convening of another meeting of heads of state to emphasize that corruption will not be tolerated.

This meeting was followed by a meeting of ministers and senior officials from Benin, Botswana, Ethiopia, Ghana, Malawi, Mali, Mozambique, Senegal, South Africa, Tanzania, and Uganda in Washington, D.C., on February 23, 1999. At the end of this meeting, the participating officials approved and adopted Principles to Combat Corruption in African Countries.[350] The principles (25 in all) set out actions that African governments should take to combat corruption. These include establishment of budgetary and financial transparency and strong financial management systems; elimination of conflicts of interest by the adoption and enforcement of effective national laws, guidelines, ethical regulations, or codes of conduct for public officials; promotion of transparency in procedures for public procurement; establishment and enforcement of self-regulatory codes of conduct for different professions, including those in the private sector; appropriate measures to ensure that anticorruption agencies are autonomous, independent, and effectively empowered to pursue investigations; and consideration of the elaboration of an African convention for combating corruption based on these principles. These principles deal with a number of issues that are being discussed in other regional and international forums, and are similar in content to the Lima Declaration against Corruption.[351]

Efforts at the Nongovernmental Level

The Lima Declaration against Corruption. The International Conference on Anticorruption in Lima, Peru, in September 1997 was the first attempt by states, nongovernmental organizations, and representatives of civil society to discuss openly the subject of bribery and corruption. The conference was attended by citizens of 93 developed and developing countries and included representatives of governments and the private sector as well as private citizens. At the end of a full week of discussion, the participants adopted the Lima Declaration against Corruption on September 11, 1997.

After noting that corruption erodes the moral fabric of every society, undermining democracy, subverting the rule of law, and retarding the development of societies, particularly among the poor, the declaration called for governments, international and regional organizations, and ordinary citizens to take specific actions for the control and possible eradication of corruption.

At the international and regional levels, the Lima Declaration called for the recognition of the creative role that civil society can play in the fight against corruption and noted, as other instruments referred to in this study have provided, that tax deductibility of bribes paid in connection with international transactions should be outlawed. It called on various international institutions, such as the OECD, World Bank, International Monetary Fund, European Union, World Trade Organization, INTERPOL, International Chamber of Commerce, and World Customs Organization, to take actions within their respective mandates and spheres of influence and, in particular, to cooperate in the suppression of corruption.[352]

At the national and local levels, states are asked to operate in a transparent and accountable manner in all activities and, more significantly, to improve the effectiveness of their laws dealing with corruption by introducing several new concepts, so long as they are consistent with constitutions and international human rights norms. Among the suggested actions are "abolishing any requirement to prove that an official who received an illegal gift actually gave favors in return,"[353] requiring those who have declared assets to justify increases that are out of line with legitimate sources of income (perhaps shifting the normal burden of proof in criminal cases),[354] empowering the state to seize and confiscate illicitly acquired wealth of officials found guilty of corruption,[355] and debarring convicted criminals from standing for political office and appointment to positions of trust.[356] The Lima Declaration concludes with a description of steps to make the prevention and prosecution of corrupt practices more effective.[357] These include improvement in procurement practices, including the possible blacklisting of firms involved in corruption associated with the bidding process; strengthening of codes of professional conduct for a wide variety of professions; improving campaign finance regulation; and education initiatives by governments, schools, and religious institutions.[358]

The International Chamber of Commerce. Another effort to adopt multilateral standards designed to influence the activities of multinational corporations was undertaken under the auspices of the International Chamber of Commerce (ICC). After work undertaken by an ad hoc commission under the chairmanship of Lord Shawcross, in 1978, the ICC issued rules that were to be applicable to international business transactions.[359] The basic purpose of the rules was to address issues of extortion and bribery in international business transactions and encourage the business community to voluntarily apply high standards of business ethics to ensure growth of international business within a framework of fair competition. The rules also suggested that governments should review their statutes relevant to extortion and bribery and take steps to effectively prohibit "all aspects of both giving bribes, as well as so-called facilitating payments to expedite the performance of functions which governmental officials have a duty to perform."[360] These rules were widely circulated, but, judging from the nature of recent amendments to them, their effect on the business community could not have been substantial. Thus, in March 1996, with the increased attention to these issues, the ICC strengthened the earlier rules and urged greater action against corruption at both the national and international levels. It is interesting to note that although these rules appeal to public international organizations to take measures to combat corruption, they basically address the behavior of ICC-member corporations. They prohibit corruption in a broad sense, which includes extortion, bribery, kickbacks, payments to agents that represent more than the appropriate remuneration for legitimate services, and contributions to political parties or committees or to individual politicians if undisclosed and made in violation of applicable laws.[361] Moreover, the rules require proper financial recording and auditing by the enterprises and require them to introduce control and review procedures within such enterprises to ensure compliance and sanctions against any director or employee responsible for contravening the rules. For whatever it is worth, despite their less formal and legally nonbinding nature, these rules of ethical business conduct undoubtedly contribute to the fight against corruption by raising the awareness of these issues among the international business community.

Conclusion. International interest in the issue of corruption has grown considerably in recent decades. Recognition of the crime of corruption has become important, and one of the crucial items on the development agenda worldwide. In addition, there is now near-unanimity of opinion that by distorting international competition, corruption has a negative effect on international business transactions. Common traits run through the bevy of recommendations, declarations, resolutions, agreements, and conventions.

First, all states are asked to take more seriously this issue of corruption and to promulgate appropriate legislation to combat it. In this connection, there appears to be even a willingness to make some changes in the procedural aspects of prosecutions—namely, shifting the burden of proof to the accused in some cases and in effect challenging the presumption that a party is innocent unless proven guilty. The willingness to move in this direction appears to be, however, mainly in connection with the crime of illicit enrichment.

Second, it is clearly recognized, at least for the developing countries, that corruption is a systemic issue that needs to be confronted in a broad-based fashion. All governmental functions need to be transparent. In particular, states need to put into place mechanisms that will ensure transparency and accountability within government, such as clear, unambiguous, and improved procurement procedures with very little discretionary authority given to government officials.

Third, there is a move in many countries, especially those within the OECD, to deny the tax deductibility of illegal kickbacks or bribes to foreign public officials.

Fourth, the proposition that concerted action by the international community may yield tangible results has been broadly accepted. This has improved government-to-government cooperation in the fight against corruption through the sharing of information on alleged offenders and the possibility, more than ever, that an alleged offender may be subject to extradition.

Finally, the role of multilateral institutions, such as the World Bank and the International Monetary Fund, in taking actions within their respective mandates to assist in the fight against corruption has been firmly recognized and encouraged.

V
Conclusion

The combat against corruption raises difficult challenges, legal and otherwise. As this comparative review of selected domestic and international legal initiatives has demonstrated, many interesting legal initiatives have been launched or are underway. Some have produced tangible results—others, less so. But legal initiatives are mere tools in the fight against corruption. History demonstrates that the most successful initiatives are those backed up by the necessary political will to fight corruption, coupled with the necessary resources to engage in and sustain the fight. No amount of rhetoric, declarations, and even legislation will have the necessary impact unless there is strong political will and the desire to improve the monitoring and enforcement capacities in all countries.

This study has attempted to review the approaches used in some of the major legal systems in the world in the fight against corruption. The analysis indicates that no single approach would be sufficient to deal effectively with this issue: a combination of the preventive and curative approaches is clearly needed. Also, bold steps must be taken to introduce new notions that should be included in the definition of corruption in a constantly changing and sophisticated world. These legal initiatives will go a long way toward dealing with this intractable problem.

This study demonstrates that for any legal initiative to have a chance of achieving its objectives, requisite political and societal will needs to be present. This is especially the case when these new initiatives have the effect of taking away long-standing and revered fundamental human rights. There is also much to be learned from experiences in the respective legal systems, which should serve as guides in any legal reform program to assist in abating corruption in any particular country. In this connection, the common elements to be considered in the development of criminal legislation with respect to bribery and corruption proposed by the OECD and dealt with by the Council of Europe offer themselves as notable examples. It is also evident from the analysis that the existence of procurement legislation that includes clear, transparent, and monitorable mechanisms, and which is devoid of discretionary powers, is desirable. Such mechanisms should ensure that processes used by states are fair, open, and competitive. This is particularly relevant in developing countries, where the main avenue for corruption often lies in the area of public procurement. In this connection, the UNCITRAL model law offers the appropriate framework for the development of such a law. Also, in this era in which the winds of democracy are blowing worldwide, the importance of laws to protect the transparency of the electoral and political process cannot be overemphasized. In this vein, there is need to promulgate appropriate legislation to regulate contributions to political parties and establish campaign spending and contribution limits that are not only transparent, but strictly audited.

However, corruption cannot be wiped out by legislative means alone, and it will continue to exist and be attempted in every state, as John Gray foresaw in 1738. In terms of its effect on international business transactions, it can be abated only if the cooperation among states, both developing and developed, continues to be strengthened. Within states, much action remains to be taken after careful analysis of what has worked or is working in terms of the legal mechanisms in existence in the world.

Endnotes

1. Sarassoro, Hyacinthe Cabago. 1990. «*La Corruption et l'enrichissement sans cause en Afrique aujourd'hui.*» *Afrique Contemporaine* (Paris) 156(4th quarter):195.

2. For example, *see* Mauro, Paulo. 1996. "The Effects of Corruption on Growth, Investment, and Government Expenditure." p. 1–27. Washington D.C.: IMF. *See also* Kofi, Tetteh A. 1995. "Corruption, Perverse Capital Accumulation and Underdevelopment in Africa." IMF Working Paper presented at the Seventh International Anticorruption Conference, Beijing, China, October 6–10. 1995.

3. *See, generally,* Goode, Richard. 1984. *Government Finance in Developing Countries*, pp. 310–11. Washington, D.C.: Brookings Institution. *See also* Paul, Samuel. 1997. "Corruption: Who Will Bell the Cat?" *Economic and Political Weekly* (June 7):1350.

4. On March 15, 1999, amid allegations of cronyism, nepotism, fraud, and corruption, the entire membership of the European Commission announced its resignation *en masse*. The resignation of the 20 members of the commission followed the release of a report of an independent panel of five auditors, which accused them of tolerating widespread fraud, corruption, and mismanagement. The report has singled out the president of the commission, a former French Prime Minister, and four other members as having engaged in or failed to prevent the hiring of friends and relatives for nonexistent jobs, and for failing to account for massive misspending in European Union programs. Other allegations noted in the report concern the recruitment of the wives of two commissioners and the brother-in-law of a third to high-level positions. *See* 1999, March 16. "EU Executive Body to Resign in Fraud Probe." *The Washington Post. See also* 1999, March 17. "EU Officials Show Little Remorse Following En Masse Resignation." *The Washington Post.*

5. Following the decision of the International Olympic Committee (IOC) in 1995 to award the 2002 winter Olympic games to Salt Lake City, Utah, there has been a series of embarrassing revelations involving cash payments, jobs, scholarships, and even land deals and escort services provided by Salt Lake Olympic Committee (SLOC) officials to IOC members

to influence the site selection process. Several local Olympic officials have since resigned or been fired in the wake of the scandal. If ever there was a blatant case of corruption, the Olympic scandal in Salt Lake City provides the classic example. Mindful of its potentially harmful ramifications, several agencies in the United States, including the Federal Bureau of Investigation, the Internal Revenue Service, the U.S. Customs Service, and the SLOC's ethics panel, as well as the IOC itself, have launched their separate investigations of the scandal. (*See* "The Olympic Scandal: Go for the Greed," *Newsweek*, January 25, 1999.) After the resignation or firing of local Olympic officials, city officials have sought to contain the damage by pinning most of the blame on their former colleagues. Meanwhile, the IOC president has claimed ignorance of the "greedy habits" of his colleagues and vowed to stay on in office. Similarly, Salt Lake City officials have indicated that they have no intention whatsoever of relinquishing their much-coveted and hard-won prize of hosting the winter Olympic games in 2002. By all accounts, the Olympic spirit is not the only lure of the games. They also bring with them millions of dollars in revenue, tourism, and new infrastructure, which no government, no matter how rich or powerful, would lightly dismiss on account of a corruption scandal. (*See also* "Blame Rolls Downhill: New Salt Lake Sins," *Newsweek*, February 15, 1999.)

6. Each and every discipline uses its own parameters to define corruption. Economists tend to define corruption from the perspective of supply and demand, or the market; political scientists tend to define it in relation to the exercise of power and of outsiders' influence on public offices; sociologists define corruption in terms of social relationship represented in the violation of socially accepted norms of duty and welfare. Similarly, while a public administration specialist will be more concerned with bureaucratic corruption, business organizations will treat corruption simply as a trade and investment policy issue. For more detail on the different perspectives on corruption, *see* Shihata, Ibrahim F. I. 1996. "Corruption: A General Review with an Emphasis on the Role of the World Bank." Paper presented at Jesus College, Cambridge, U.K., September 9, pp. 1–6.

7. For details on the World Bank perspective and involvement in combating corruption, *see* World Bank. 1997. *Helping Countries to Combat Corruption. The Role of the World Bank*, p. 8. Washington, D.C. *See generally*, World Bank. 1994. *Governance. The World Bank Experience. Development in Practice*. Washington, D.C.

8. According to experts, there are three forms of corruption: *collusive* (involving willing and planned cooperation of the giver and the taker), *extortionary* (implying forced extraction of bribes or other favors from vul-

nerable victims by the authority), and *anticipatory* (involving payment of a bribe or presentation of a gift in anticipation of favorable actions or decisions). *See* Paul, *supra* note 3, p. 1351. For additional detail on techniques to conduct corrupt acts, *see also* World Bank, 1997, *Helping Countries to Combat Corruption*, pp. 8–20.

9. *See, generally*, Gray, Cheryl W., and Daniel Kauffmann. 1998. "Corruption and Development." *Finance and Development* (March):7–10.

10. *See, generally* Gray and Kauffmann 1998; *see also* Rose-Ackerman, Susan. 1997. "The Political Economy of Corruption." In Kimberly Ann Elliott, ed., *Corruption and the Global Economy*, pp. 3–56. Washington, D.C.: Institute for International Economics. *See also* Mauro 1996, pp. 83–105.

11. Ghana Constitution (1992), Article 35.8. Entered into force on January 7, 1993.

12. Nepal Constitution (1991), Article 97(1).

13. Nepal Constitution, Article 98(1).

14. Nepal Constitution, Article 97(2).

15. Uganda Constitution (1995), Article XXVI. *See also* the Ugandan Leadership Code (1991), Statute N.8.

16. The legal basis for combating corruption in Ukraine was further strengthened by the law introduced by the Verkhovna Rada's (Parliament) Resolution No. 357-95-BP (the Law on the Combat Against Corruption, October 5, 1995). The law defines corruption as an "activity of persons authorized to perform state functions, aiming at illicit usage of their authority for receiving material benefits, services, privileges and other advantages." The "persons authorized to perform state functions" include civil servants and members of the parliament of Ukraine.

17. In 1996, Pakistan promulgated the Accountability Ordinance. Its objective is to provide for the eradication of corruption by public officials as well as provide effective measures for prosecution and speedy disposal of cases involving corruption. In substance, the Accountability Ordinance applies to every holder of public office, with a focus on higher-ranking members of the bureaucracy and legislatures at both the federal and provincial levels. It brings within its purview not only those presently hold-

ing certain public offices, but also those who held such public offices in
the past. While the application of the Accountability Ordinance is limited
to senior officials and legislators in terms of the practices that it sanctions,
its coverage is extensive. The ordinance relies on a broad definition of the
term "corruption and corrupt practices," using it to include not just financial corruption (acquisition of property by illegal or unfair [noncontrac-
tual] means or through abuse of power), but political corruption
(committing or causing rigging of elections) as well. For a more detailed
discussion of the Ordinance, *see* Hassan, T. 1997, November 13. "Corruption and Accountability in Pakistan." http:/www.erols.com/ziqbal/
corrup.htm.

18. The Lima Declaration against Corruption (September 11, 1997) referred to this as "cleaning a staircase by starting at the top." For details of
the Lima Declaration, *see* notes 351 and 352 and accompanying text.

19. Such provisions are found, for instance, in the Tanzanian Public
Leadership Code of Ethics N.13 (1995) (An Act to Establish a Code of Ethics for Certain Public Leaders to Provide for the Organization of the Ethics
Secretariat and for Matters Connected with or Incidental to Them), and
the Ugandan Leadership Code Statute (1991), N.8.

20. Ghana Constitution, Article 286(1).

21. Ghana Constitution, Article 286(3). The Commissioner is empowered to investigate all instances of alleged or suspected corruption and
misappropriation of public monies by officials (see Article 218(e)).

22. Ghana Constitution, Article 286(4).

23. This is complemented by the Leadership Code Statute of 1991, which
requires annual declarations of income, assets, and liabilities by leaders.
The code specifies minimum behavior and conduct standards for leaders
regarding gifts and benefits in kind, as well as interests in contracts and
tenders and the use or abuse of public property. *See* Langseth, Petter,
Damien Kato, Mohammad Kisubi, and Jeremy Pope. 1997. "Good Governance in Africa: A Case Study of Uganda," p. 17. Economic Development
Institute Working Paper, World Bank. Washington, D.C.

24. Turkish Constitution 1982 (as amended), Chapter IV, Part 2, Article.
71 (on the right to enter the public service).

25. Mozambique Ethics Law, March 1998.

26. Ethics in Government Act 1978, Pub. L. No. 95-521, 92 Stat. 1824.

27. *See* Section 3 A(2).

28. Declaration of Assets Act 1991, Sections 3(1) and 3(2).

29. Declaration of Assets Act, Section 3(3).

30. Prevention of Corruption Act (Chapter 241 Statutes, Law of 1952–1993 Revision).

31. *See, generally,* Pope, Jeremy. 1995. "Containing Corruption in International Transactions. The Challenges of the 1990s. In *Issue in Global Governance,* p. 73. Commission on Global Governance. London:Kluwer Law International.

32. Olowu, Dale, and Victor Ayeni. 1998. "Public Service Accountability in Nigeria." In Joseph G. Jabbra and O .P. Dwivedi, eds., *Public Service Accountability: A Comparative Perspective,* p. 149. Connecticut: Kumarian Press.

33. Paul 1997, p. 1355.

34. *See* de Speville, Bertrand. 1997. "Reversing the Onus of Proof: Is it Compatible with Respect for Human Rights Norms?, p. 9. Paper circulated at the 8th International Anti-Corruption Conference, September 7-11, Lima, Peru). *See also, for instance,* Section 17(2) of the Malaysian Prevention of Corruption Act 1961.

35. *See also generally,* Paul 1997, pp. 1350–55.

36. Wiltshire, Kenneth. 1988. "Accountability in the Australian Public Service." In Joseph G. Jabbra and O. P. Dwivedi, eds., *Public Service Accountability: A Comparative Perspective,* p. 106. Connecticut: Kumarian Press.

37. Ghana Constitution, Chapter 24.

38. Ghana Constitution, Article 284.

39. Ghana Constitution, Article 286(5). The public offices to which the provision applies are those of: the President of the Republic, the Vice President of the Republic, the speaker, the deputy speaker and members of parliament, minister of state or deputy minister, chief justice, justice of the

superior court of judicature, chairman of a regional tribunal, the commissioner for human rights and administrative justice and his deputies and all judicial officers, ambassador or high commissioner, secretary to the cabinet, head of ministry or government department or equivalent office in the civil service, chairman, managing director, general manager and departmental head of public corporation or company in which the state has a controlling interest, and such officers in the public service and any other public institution as parliament may prescribe.

40. *See, generally,* Tashiro, Ku. 1988. "Accountability in the Public Service: A Comparative Perspective in Japan." In Joseph G. Jabbra and O. P. Dwivedi, eds., *Public Service Accountability: A Comparative Perspective,* p. 218. Connecticut: Kumarian Press.

41. The rationale for making illegal the demand or acceptance of gifts and benefits by public officials in return for, or in connection with, the performance of their official functions, is important. Giving or receiving gifts is a practice deeply rooted in the culture of many societies. As noted emphatically by the Constitutional Commission of Ghana in connection with the drafting of Ghana's 1978 constitution, a prevailing belief is that something must be done to stop the transformation of a once laudable practice into a shameless machinery and pretext for open and serious corruption and graft. This has led many countries to incorporate provisions accordingly in their legal framework. *See* "The Proposals of the Constitutional Commission for a Constitution for the Establishment of a Transitional (Interim) National Government for Ghana" (1978), Accra, Ghana, pp. 117–21 (in connection with the drafting of that constitution). According to the Constitutional Commission,

> it is now difficult to accept that, as the practice is so rampant and deep-rooted in some societies, no attempt should be made to bring it under some control. Certainly, it is difficult to abolish altogether the giving and receiving of gifts as genuine tokens of gratitude for kindnesses or courtesies shown. But the existence of clear provisions against the giving and receiving of gifts and benefits which are clearly intended to influence public officers to take measures or adopt procedures not permitted by the applicable rules or regulations can serve as a deterrent and a standing warning and reminder to all public officers.

For detailed discussions of the rationale for having code of conduct, *see* "The Proposals," pp. 117–21.

42. The Congressional Ethics Code is indeed detailed. For instance, the gift rules applicable to the House of Representatives prohibit any

member, officer, or employee of the House of Representatives from knowingly accepting a gift. As per the rule, the term "gift" means any gratuity, favor, discount, entertainment, hospitality, loan, forbearance, or other item having monetary value. The term includes gifts of services, training, transportation, lodging, and meals, whether provided in kind, by purchase of a ticket, payment in advance, or reimbursement after the expense has been incurred. Similarly, a gift to a family member of a member, officer, or employee of the House of Representatives, or a gift to any other individual based on that individual's relationship with the member, officer, or employee, shall be considered a gift to the member, officer, or employee if it is given with his or her knowledge and acquiescence and the member, officer, or employee has reason to believe the gift was given because of his or her official position. The scope of the rule extends even to hospitality: If food or refreshment is provided at the same time and place to both a member, officer, or employee and his or her spouse or dependent, only the food or refreshment provided to the member, officer, or employee shall be treated as a gift.

43. On Competition and the Restriction of Monopolistic Activities in Commodity Markets, March 21, 1991, as amended through May 25, 1995 (the Antimonopoly Law).

44. On the Foreign Travel of Officials of Central Federal Bodies of the Executive Branch, July 2, 1993 (Decree No. 981).

45. As a result of the allegations of cronyism, nepotism, fraud, and corruption that have plagued the European Commission during the early part of 1999, the President of the Commission has installed an ethics code for commissioners that prohibits them from running for office in their home countries while they are employed by the European Commission in Brussels, accepting outside income, and using personal influence in recruitment matters. *See* "EU Executive Body to Resign in Fraud Probe" 1999, March 16, p. *See also* 1999, March 17. "A Day After Resigning, Some European Commissioners Have Second Thoughts." *The Washington Post*, The new ethics rules notwithstanding, there is at least one commissioner, according to *The Washington Post*, who is running for the presidency in the commissioner's own country.

46. *See* Ministerial Code. A Code of Conduct and Guidance on Procedures for Ministers, United Kingdom, 1997 (U.K. Code).

47. *See* U.K. Code, 1997.

48. *See, for further details*, the Aitken case, *infra* note 52 and accompanying text.

49. The U.K. Code is elaborate and comprises provisions that are not always necessarily related to financial corruption proper, but also to other aspects of political governance. For instance, the ministers are to make the most important announcements of government policy in the first instance in Parliament and are to consult with law officers in good time before the government is committed to critical decisions requiring legal consideration. Moreover, the U.K. Code specifies that the prime minister is responsible for the overall organization of the executive branch and the allocation of functions between ministers in charge of departments. As a result, the prime minister's written approval should be sought wherever changes are proposed that affect the allocation of responsibilities for the discharge of ministerial functions. The U.K. Code also provides guidance to ministers to enable them to carry out their functions without any conflict of interest, and provides detailed rules governing the relationships between ministers and the Crown, ministers and the government, ministers and the parliament, ministers and their departments, and ministers and the civil service.

50. The U.K. Code provides detailed guidance on the relationship between ministers and civil servants. It indicates, among other things, that in reaching policy decisions, it is the duty of ministers to give fair consideration and due weight to informed and impartial advice from civil servants, as well as to other considerations and advice. It also provides for a duty to observe the obligations of a good employer with regard to terms and conditions of those of who serve them.

51. In this connection, a recent case is noteworthy. Alan Meale, the U.K. Minister of Environment, was accused of breaching the U.K. Code after lobbying his own department to promote a £14 million scheme that would benefit Tony Kleanthouse, with whom he had a personal friendship. During questioning by the press, the minister was invited to explain his behavior in light of the U.K. Code. Somewhat curiously, his response was that he was unaware of its very existence. *See.* 1998, November 1. "Minister Gave Millionaire Party Donor a Commons Pass." *The Sunday Times* (London). *See also* 1998, November 1. "Meale and the Men Who Profited from Friendship." *The Sunday Times* (London).

52. Another fairly recent case in London involving a former minister, Jonathan Aitken, is a case in point. In 1993, while he was defense procurement minister, Aitken was alleged to have allowed an Arab friend pay his

hotel bill in the Paris Ritz. He was later charged with conspiracy, perjury, and perverting the course of justice. The hospitality Aitken enjoyed appears to have been in clear violation of Paragraph 126 of the U.K. Code. Paradoxically, however, his tribulations arose not as a result of any criminal action, but after he tried and failed to use a libel suit to disprove allegations of impropriety made against him by a newspaper. His was a personal tragedy brought about not so much by any sophisticated anticorruption legislation, but by a basic rule of conduct coupled with the power and tenacity of a free press. In other countries, the journalists might have been hounded, intimidated, and even thrown in jail for their embarrassing revelations. In the United Kingdom, the matter was left to be decided by the courts, whose verdict left little room for doubt about the course of events that precipitated Aitken's downfall. The case provides important lessons, not just about the practical application of codes of conduct but also in terms of the role of the media, which is the subject of the next section of this study. *See, for more detail,* Carroll, Rory. 1998, September 16. "Aitken in Dock over Libel Case." *The Guardian. See* also Jones, Tim. 1998, September 16. "Aitken in Court to Face Perjury Charge." *The Times* (London).

53. *See Déontologie des magistrats, Circulaire* No. 57-MJ/CAB (June 30, 1997).

54. The Code of Conduct for United States Judges. Most state courts in the United States have adopted the abbreviated version of the Judicial Canons recommended by the American Bar Association. *See* Ashman, Charles R. 1973. *The Finest Judges Money Can Buy and Other Forms of Judicial Pollution,* pp. 279, 280–96.

55. Code of Conduct for United States Judges, Canon 6.

56. Code of Conduct for United States Judges, Canon 6.

57. Commentaries, Code of Conduct for United States Judges, Canon 6.

58. *See, generally,* Paul 1997, pp. 1350–55.

59. The Japanese press, for instance, is believed to conceive its mission as involving systematic and continuous criticism of the government in power. *See* Ward, Robert E. 1978. *Japan's Political System,* 2nd ed., p. 52. Englewood Cliffs, N.J.: Prentice-Hall.

60. *See* Tashiro 1988, p. 219. It should also be noted that in the United States, as in European or Asian countries, major corruption scandals have

come to light as a result of the vigilance and determination of a free and dynamic press.

61. *See* Padgett, George E. 1980. "A Quantitative Analysis of United States Supreme Court Decision-Making Relative to First Amendment Issues of Free Speech and Free Press," p. 1. Ph.D. diss. Ohio University.

62. Ghana Constitution, Chapter 12, Articles 162–65.

63. Ghana Constitution, Chapter 12, Articles 166–73.

64. Nigeria Constitution, Article 21.

65. Sakal Papers V. India, AIR 1962 SC 305, cited in Jain, M. P. 1987. *Indian Constitutional Law*, 4th ed., p. 527. Bombay: N. M. Tripathi Ltd.

66. *See* Jain 1987, p. 527.

67. *See, for details*, Pember, Don R. 1977. *Mass Media Law*. Dubuque, Iowa: Brown Company. In whistleblowing cases, there is always a tension between the severe private costs to an individual and the benefit of whistleblowing to the community at large. Because of the significant contribution whistleblowers can make, the society should devise a reasonable protection system for them. Apart from the protection granted in the context of the freedom of the media, in 1988, a Whistleblower Protection Bill passed in the U.S. Senate and House unanimously. However, the bill was vetoed by President Reagan. *See, for detail,* Glazer, Myron Peretz, and Penina Migdal Glazer. 1989. Whistleblowers: Exposing Corruption in Government and Industry, pp. 250—51. New York: Basic Books Inc. Many states in the United States have promulgated whistleblower laws with the purpose of protecting persons reporting violations of law. In essence, these laws stipulate that a state agency or local government may not suspend or terminate the employment of, or discriminate against, a public employer who in good faith reports a violation of law to an appropriate law enforcement authority.

68. For additional detail on different shield laws protecting journalists' confidential sources, *see* Dill, Barbara. 1986. The Journalist's Handbook on Libel and Privacy, pp. 242–44. New York: Free Press.

69. Dill 1986, pp. 242–44.

70. *See, generally*, Rowat, Donald C., ed. 1979. *Administrative Secrecy in Developed Countries*, p. 1. New York: Columbia University Press.

71. *See* Holstad, Sigvard. 1979. "Sweden."In Donald C. Rowat, ed., *Administrative Secrecy in Developed Countries*, p. 29. New York: Columbia University Press.

72. *See, generally*, Carter, Lief H. 1983. *Administrative Law and Politics: Cases and Comments*, p. 107. Boston: Little, Brown and Company. For the problem regarding interpretation of the scope of the categories of exemption and the American case law, *see* Carter 1983, p. 108.

73. The FOIA applies to records maintained by agencies within the executive branch of the federal government, including the Executive Office of the President and independent regulatory agencies. Records maintained by state governments, municipal corporations, the courts, Congress, or citizens are not included.

74. Uganda Constitution, Article 41.

75. Nepal Constitution, Article16.

76. Some countries require several layers of legal instruments. Article 57 of the Senegal Constitution, for instance, requires that the finance laws be voted in the National Assembly in accordance with an organic law. Moreover, an organic law on national resources, debt services, and accounting allocation, and the law pertaining to the Ministry of Finance, treasury, tax and customs, financial control, inspectorate general, auditor general, and numerous other rules and regulations detailing several aspects thereof, are also relevant in ensuring the implementation of the financial management system in Senegal. An approach more or less similar to the one in Senegal is common to most West African countries with civil law traditions.

77. *See, for detail*, Mikesell, R. M., and Leon. E. Hay. 1961. *Governmental Accounting*, p. 3. Homewood, Illinois: Richard D. Irwin Inc.

78. U.S. Federal Financial Management Act of 1994, Title 31 of the United States Code (Financial Management Act).

79. The Office of the Management and Budget is an office in the Executive Office of the President. *See* Financial Management Act, Section 501.

80. Financial Management Act, Section 3515.

81. *See* Financial Management Act, Section 3515.

82. Financial Management Act, Section 331(e).

83. *See, generally,* Financial Management Act, Section 331.

84. For instance, in the United States, pursuant to Section 703 of the Financial Management Act, the Comptroller General is appointed by the president, by and with the advice and consent of the Senate.

85. *See, for details,* Weston, Martin. 1991. *An English Reader's Guide to the French Legal System,* pp. 89–90. New York: St. Martin's Press.

86. According to a recent frontpage newspaper report, the list of party donors compiled for presentation to the Labor Party conference in the fall of 1998 was bound to reignite controversy over allegations of cash for favors. Although there are no laws requiring disclosure of political contributions in Britain, the Labor Party appeared to have taken the initiative to publish the names of those donors who contributed in excess of £5,000. *See* Brennan, Zoe, and Jonathan Carr-Brown. 1998, August 30. "Labor Donors Trigger Cash-for-Favors Row." *The Sunday Times* (London). *See also* Lowrie, Margaret. 1997, April 4. "In Britain, Keeping Campaign Finances Secret Is No Crime." *CNN World News Report.*

87. Ortiz, Daniel R. 1998. "The Democratic Paradox of Campaign Finance Reform." 50 *Stanford Law. Review,* 893, 897—901.

88. U.K.: Representation of the People Act 1983, Section 76.

89. U.K.: Representation of the People Act 1983, Section 75(1).

90. U.K.: Representation of the People Act 1983, Section 75(2).

91. U.K.: Representation of the People Act 1983, Section 81.

92. U.K.: Representation of the People Act 1983, Section 89.

93. Mauritius: Representation of the People Act (1958), Section 51.

94. Mauritius: Representation of the People Act, Section 56.

95. Mauritius: Representation of the People Act, Section 52.

96. Mauritius: Representation of the People Act, Section 55(1).

97. Mauritius: Representation of the People Act, Section 55(2).

98. *See* Mauritius: Representation of the People Act, Section 55(2).

99. Mauritius: Representation of the People Act, Section 52.

100. U.S.: Federal Election Campaigns Act (FECA), 2 U.S.C. 431–442 (1994).

101. Karl Rove & Co. v. Thornburgh (C.A.5 Tex. 1994), 39 F.3d 1273; Orloski v. FEC (C.A.D.C. 1986), 795 F.2d 156, 254 U.S. App. D.C. 111.

102. FEC v. National Republican Senatorial Committee (D. D.C. 1991), 761 F.Supp.813.

103. U.S.: FECA, , 2 U.S.C. Sections 431–442, 441a(a)(1)(A) (1994).

104. U.S.: FECA, 2 U.S.C. Section 441a(a)(3) (1994).

105. U.S.: FECA, 2 U.S.C. Section 441a(a)(1), (2) (1994).

106. In the United Kingdom, foreign contributions are not just lawful; according to some reports, they are actively encouraged. In the period from 1992 to 1997, at least 6 of 17 donations of more than £1 million received by the Conservative Party came from overseas. *See* "New Rules for Campaign Finance." 1998, October 17–23. *The Economist*, p. 61.

107. U.S.: FECA, 2 U.S.C. Sections 431–442, 441(e) (1994).

108. Buckley v. Valeo, 424 U.S. 1 (1976).

109. Ayres, Ian, and Jeremy Bulow. "The Donation Booth: Mandating Donor Anonymity to Disrupt the Market for Political Influence." 1998. 50 *Stanford Law Review*, 844, 893.

110. The purpose of the Bill is to curtail the indiscriminate use of the so-called "soft money" contributions of political parties, by providing a detailed definition of such contributions and the purposes to which they can be applied. It seeks to expand the scope of "express advocacy," a regulated form of political speech designed to advocate the election or the defeat of particular candidates, by providing a more comprehensive definition of the term, and one that does not rely on the use of any magic words to convey support for such advocacy. In so doing, the Bill seeks conversely to

narrow the scope for issue advocacy, an unregulated form of political speech intended to promote specific issues of general importance that has also been used to great effect to expressly advocate the election of particular candidates. Finally, the Bill proposes detailed definitions of the terms "independent expenditures" and "coordinated expenditures" and goes on to draw a sharp dividing line between the two types of expenditures, both for reporting purposes and for the purposes of campaign expenditures made by political parties.

111. According to a *Washington Post* editorial, soft money was the source of most of the fund-raising abuses in the 1996 election. The Republicans denounced the practice, but then went on to block the legislation that would have forbidden it. They love the issue, according to the editorial, but they love the money even more. The *Post* concluded that the Catch 22 of campaign finance is that the power to change the system rests with precisely the people it has helped to elect. *See* "A Campaign Finance Breakout." 1998, October 29. *The Washington Post*, p. A26.

112 Dalloz. 1998. *Codes éditions périodiques: Code électoral*, Articles L.52-4–L.52-18.

113. Dalloz 1998, Article L.52-11.

114. Dalloz 1998, Article L.52-8, Paragraph 1.

115. Dalloz 1998, Article L.52-8, Paragraph 2.

116. Dalloz 1998, Article L.52-8, Paragraph 4.

117. Dalloz 1998, L.52-8, Paragraph 3.

118. Dalloz 1998, Article L.52-8, Paragraph 5.

119. Dalloz 1998, 136–143.

120. Dalloz 1998, 126–136.

121. Dalloz 1998, 139, Paragraph 7.

122. Dalloz 1998, 139, Paragraph 2.

123. Dalloz 1998, 139, Paragraph 1.

124. Dalloz 1998, 133, Paragraph 38.

125. Dalloz 1998, 129, Paragraphs 1, 2.

126. Dalloz 1998, Article L.52-15, Paragraph 1.

127. Dalloz 1998, Article L.52-15, Paragraph 3.

128. Dalloz 1998, Article L.52-15, Paragraph 4.

129. After the Labor Party victory in the last general elections in the United Kingdom, the new Labor government appointed the Committee on Standards in Public Life, headed by Lord Neill, to re-examine the issue of funding of political parties. The committee, which delivered its report recently, has made a number of drastic recommendations on campaign financing that are currently under review. The committee's report called for a ban on foreign donations and a modest increase in public funding for political parties, as well as tax relief measures to encourage small donations of up to £500. Although the committee did not wish to set any limit on individual donations, it has urged the government to take action to have all donations of more than £5,000 swiftly declared. The committee has also recommended a limit of £20 million on total expenditures by any political party during an election, as well as a limit of £1 million on spending by third parties. *See* "New Rules for Campaign Finance." 1998, October 17–23. *The Economist*, p. 61–2.

130. Article 217(1) of the Constitution of South Africa provides as follows: "When an organ of state in the national, provincial or local sphere of government, or any other institution identified in national legislation, contracts for goods and services, it must do so in accordance with a system which is fair, equitable, transparent, competitive and cost-effective."

131. France: *Code des marchés publics,* Decree No. 64-729 of July 17, 1964, as amended, among others, by Decree No. 91-1232, December 6, 1991; Decree No. 92-1310, December 15, 1992; and Decree No. 94-334, April 27, 1994 [French *Code des marchés publics*].

132. Mali: *Décret portant règlementation des marchés publics,* Decree No. 92-059, February 14, 1992 [Mali: *Décret portant règlementation de marchés publics*].

133. United Nations. 1995. UNCITRAL Model Law on Procurement of Goods, Construction and Services [UNCITRAL Model Law], with Guide to Enactment. New York.

134. Guide to Enactment 1995, Paragraph 3.

135. Guide to Enactment, Paragraph 1.

136. Ministry of Economy of the Republic of Latvia. 1995, November 27. Draft Law on Public Procurement [Latvia: Draft Law on Public Procurement].

137. In the case of states with civil law tradition, the constitution usually prescribes a list of matters that are within the exclusive province of the national assembly and in respect of which formal legislation is required (*domaine réservé de la loi*). Matters not so reserved to be under the exclusive legislative authority of the national assembly may be regulated by decree.

138. Mauritius: Central Tender Board Act (Act 39 of 1994), December 29, 1994.

139. Guide to Enactment, Paragraph 8.

140. Madagascar: Decree No. 91-056, January 29, 1991.

141. 1992. *African Public Procurement Systems, a Compendium of Public Procurement Rules and Regulations in Eleven African Countries—with a Comparative Analysis.*, p. 3. International Trade Center.

142. World Bank. 1995, January. *Guidelines for Procurement under IBRD Loans and IDA Credits*, revised January 1996, August 1996, September 1997, and January 1999 [World Bank Guidelines for the Procurement of Goods and Works]. Washington, D.C.
Procurement of services under World Bank-financed contracts is governed by World Bank. 1997, January. *Guidelines: Selection and Employment of Consultants by World Bank Borrowers*, revised September 1997 and January 1999 [World Bank Consultant Guidelines]. Washington, D.C.

143. World Bank Guidelines for the Procurement of Goods and Works, Paragraph 1.2.

144. The French *Code des marchés publics* makes a distinction between two types of competitive bidding: *marchés par adjudication* and *marchés sur appel d'offres*. The essential distinction between the two methods of procurement is that, in the first case, the award is made solely on the basis of price, while in the second case, it is usually based on price and other technical and economic criteria as may be relevant. *See* French Code, Articles.

38, 38 *bis*, and 84–97 *quater*. *See also* Mali: *Décret portant règlementation* 1992, February 14, Articles 24–46.

145. UNCITRAL Model Law 1995, Article 21.

146. UNCITRAL Model Law 1995, Article 22.

147. Mali: *Décret portant règlementation* 1992, Article. 56 requires the prior approval of the *Direction Générale des Marchés Publics* in respect of any proposal to procure on a sole-source basis.

148. UNCITRAL Model Law 1995, Articles 11(1)(i), 18(4).

149. UNCITRAL Model Law 1995, Article 11(1)(l).

150. UNCITRAL Model Law 1995, Article 6(1)(b).

151. UNCITRAL Model Law 1995, Article 3.

152. UNCITRAL Model Law 1995, Articles 3, 4.

153. UNCITRAL Model Law 1995, Article 7. *See also* Latvia: Draft Law on Public Procurement 1995, Article 5, and Mali: *Décret portant règlementation* 1992, Article 46.

154. France: *Code des marchés publics*, Articles 38, 50.

155. France: *Code des marchés publics*, Article 94 *bis*.

156. France: *Code des marchés publics*, Article 95.

157. Guide to Enactment 1995, Paragraph 16.

158. UNCITRAL Model Law 1995, Article 24.

159. UNCITAL Model Law 1995, Article 27(d). *See also* Latvia: Draft Law on Public Procurement 1995, Article 17.1.3.

160. UNCITRAL Model Law 1995, Article 27(e). *See also* Latvia: Draft Law on Public Procurement 1995, Article 17.1.4.

161. UNCITRAL Model Law 1995, Article 33(2). *See also* Latvia: Draft Law on Public Procurement 1995, Article 21.2.

162. UNCITRAL Model Law 1995, Articles 28(1)–(2), 30(2).

163. UNCITRAL Model Law 1995, Article 30(5). The double-envelope procedure, which applies in many jurisdictions, requires bidders to submit a double envelope, consisting of a sealed outer envelope, containing the details of the bidder's status and qualifications, and an inner sealed envelope containing details of the tender.

164. UNCITRAL Model Law 1995, Article 33(2). *See also* Mali: *Décret portant règlementation* 1992, Article 37, which provides for bids to be opened and read aloud in the presence of bidders or their representatives who wish to be present. By contrast the French *Code des marchés publics* has no provision for the public opening of tenders in cases of *marchés sur appel d'offres*.

165. UNCITRAL Model Law 1995, Article 34(4)(b), -(c).

166. UNCITRAL Model Law 1995, Article 27(e).

167. UNCITRAL Model Law 1995, Article 34(4)(a).

168. UNCITRAL Model Law 1995, Article 34(4)(d).

169. UNCITRAL Model Law 1995, Article 34(4)(b)(ii).

170. UNCITRAL Model Law 1995, Article 35.

171. UNCITRAL Model Law 1995, Article 35(1)(a).

172. UNCITRAL Model Law 1995, Article 35(1)(b).

173. UNCITRAL Model Law 1995, Article 35(1)(a).

174. Mali: *Décret portant règlementation* 1992, Articles 38, 40.

175. UNCITRAL Model Law 1995, Article 27(h).

176. Mali: *Décret portant règlementation* 1992, Article 53: «*Le règlement de la consultation doit indiquer: le nombre de lots, la nature de l'emplacement et la dimension de chaque lot et, le cas échéant, le nombre minimum de lots pour lesquels un soumissionaire peut présenter une offre. Un soumissionaire peut faire figurer dans son offre le rabais global qu'il consent pour la combinaison de certains lots ou de tous les lots pour lesquels il a présenté une offre distincte.*»

177. Darbyshire, Penny. 1995. "English Legal System." In *Nutshells*, 3d ed., p. 71. London: Sweet and Maxwell.

178. U.S.: Independent Counsel Statute, 28 U.S.C. 591–599.

179. U.S.: Ethics in Government Act 1978, Pub. L. No. 95-521, 92 Stat. 1824.

180. Rossbacher, Henry H., and Tracy W. Young. Spring 1997. "The Foreign Corrupt Practices Act within the American Response to Domestic Corruption." *Dickinson Journal of International Law* 15:509.

181. U.S.: Independent Counsel Statute, 28 U.S.C., Section 591(b).

182. U.S.: Independent Counsel Statute, Section 591(c)(2).

183. U.S.: Independent Counsel Statute, Section 591(a).

184. U.S.: Independent Counsel Statute, Section 591(d)(2).

185. U.S.: Independent Counsel Statute, Section 591(d)(2): preliminary investigation is mandatory if, within the 30-day period, the Attorney General determines that the information is specific and from a credible source, or even if, within that period, he has been unable to make any determination whatsoever.

186. U.S.: Independent Counsel Statute, Section 592(a)(3): the 90-day deadline is subject to a one-time extension of not more than 60 days, which the court may grant at the request of the Attorney General, and upon showing of good cause.

187. U.S.: Independent Counsel Statute, Section 592(b)(1).

188. U.S.: Independent Counsel Statute, Section 592(c)(1).

189. U.S.: Independent Counsel Statute, Section 594(a).

190. U.S.: Independent Counsel Statute, Section 595(a)(2).

191. U.S.: Independent Counsel Statute, Section 596(a)(1).

192. Among the more serious grounds of criticism that the Office of the Independent Counsel has attracted, one in particular merits attention.

It was alluded to by New York Mayor Rudolph Guiliani in remarks that he
made to *Washington Post* reporters. The independent counsel is charged
with investigating charges on the basis of a given set of circumstances. His
or her entire career often rests on the ability to establish the charges and
their outcome. *See* 1998, December 3. "Espy Case Could Spur Reform of
Independent Counsel Law." *The Washington Post. See also* "Are Independent Counsels Necessary?" 1999, March 6. *The Economist*, 21: ". . . a special
prosecutor tends now to be appointed to investigate a person rather than
a crime; and, mindful that he is spending a lot of public money and must
show some return for it, he has every incentive to investigate that person
almost to death."

193. Even though the Attorney General moved, on May 11, 1998, to
have an independent counsel appointed to investigate the conduct of Labor Secretary Alexis Herman, her request to the court did not, according
to a *Washington Post* editorial, read as if she thought that a criminal case
against Ms. Herman was likely: ". . . our investigation," she wrote, "has
developed no evidence clearly demonstrating Secretary Herman's involvement in these matters, and substantial evidence suggesting that she may
not have been involved . . . ." *See* "Another Independent Counsel." 1998,
May 13. *The Washington Post.*

194. "Are Independent Counsels Necessary?" 1999, March 6, 21.

195. Hong Kong: Independent Commission against Corruption Ordinance [ICAC Ordinance] (Chapter 204), Section 3.

196. Hong Kong: ICAC Ordinance, Section 5.

197. Hong Kong: ICAC Ordinance, Section 12.

198. For general discussions, *see, generally*, Hassan, 1997, November 13.

199. *See* Hassan, 1997, November 13.

200. Tanzania: Prevention of Corruption Act 1993 (as amended) (Chapter 329), Section 2A.

201. Malawi: Corrupt Practices Act of 1995 (No. 18 of 1995), Section 4.

202. Malawi: Corrupt Practices Act of 1995, Section 4.

203. Malawi: Corrupt Practices Act of 1995, Sections 6, 7.

204. Malawi: Corrupt Practices Act of 1995, Section 10.

205. Malawi: Corrupt Practices Act of 1995, Section 11.

206. Malawi: Corrupt Practices Act of 1995, Section 12.

207. Kenya: Prevention of Corruption Act 1965 (Chapter 65 of the laws of Kenya).

208. 1998, May 15. *The Weekly Review*.

209. Mauritius: Unified Revenue Act of 1983 (Act 59 of 1983), Section 5(1)(b).

210. Mauritius: Unified Revenue Act of 1983, Section 5(1)(d).

211. Mauritius: Unified Revenue Act of 1983, Section 5(1)(e).

212. Mauritius: Unified Revenue Act of 1983, Section 8(4).

213. Mauritius: Unified Revenue Act of 1983, Section 5(2).

214. Mauritius: Unified Revenue Act of 1983, Section 3(2).

215. "Hong Kong's Tung Tied." 1998, March 28. *The Economist*, 39. In many countries the refusal of the political leadership to prosecute an individual who has been investigated for fraud and found amenable to prosecution hardly causes a stir. In Hong Kong, according to news media, such an episode caused an uproar. According to Professor Yash Ghai of the University of Hong Kong, the commitment of the people of Hong Kong to the law may be greater than their commitment to democracy.

216. U.K.: Prevention of Corruption Act of 1889, Section 1.

217. U.K.: Prevention of Corruption Act of 1906, Section 1(1).

218. Kenya: Prevention of Corruption Act of 1956 (Cap 65).

219. U.S.: Bribery Laws, 18 U.S.C., Section 201(c)(1)(A).

220. U.S.: Bribery Laws, 18 U.S.C., Section 201(c)(1)(B). In spite of the requirement that the gift to a public official must be given "for or because of any official act" rendered, there has been some speculation, backed by

precedents, that simply giving a gift to an official in a position to make decisions affecting the giver was enough to constitute a crime. Overturning a conviction based on such precedents against Sun Diamond Growers of California, the D.C. Circuit Court of Appeals recently ruled that there must have been some official act that the gift giver benefited from, or hoped to benefit from, for the law to be breached. According to the appeals court, it was not enough for a gift to be motivated by the mere desire of the giver to ingratiate himself generally with the official. The appeals court ruling is being challenged before the U.S. Supreme Court, which is expected to give a definitive ruling in 1999. *See* 1998, November 3. "High Court to Review Espy Probe Conviction." *The Washington Post*, p. A1, A4.

Sun Diamond Growers' case is linked to the case of the former Secretary of Agriculture, Mike Espy, who was charged with accepting illegal gratuities for himself and his former girlfriend and relatives, and with violating the Meat Inspection Act of 1907, which bars Department of Agriculture employees from taking anything of value from companies they are charged with regulating. Espy has since been acquitted of all 30 counts of corruption with which he had been charged. The basis for the acquittal appears to have been that, although Espy admittedly received gifts, there had been no evidence to demonstrate that he did anything in return for them. According to *The Washington Post*, the law permits officials to receive gifts out of friendship or a desire to establish warm feelings, so long as the items are not "for or because of official acts." *See* 1998, December 3. "Ex-USDA Espy Acquitted on 30 Corruption Counts." *The Washington Post*.

221. France: *Nouveau code pénal*, Articles 432-11, 433-1.

222. Mauritius: Penal Code, Sections 126, 128.

223. U.S.: Foreign Corrupt Practices Act of 1977, 15 U.S.C., Sections 78dd-1, 78dd-2. The 1977 act, as originally enacted, required merely that a company should have "reason to know" that an improper payment was being made. After an amendment was introduced in 1988, that standard was changed to introduce a requirement of actual knowledge. A person meets this standard if he or she is aware that an improper payment is being made, the circumstances for an improper payment exist, the improper payment is substantially certain to be made, or the person has a firm belief that the circumstances exist or that the improper payment is substantially certain to occur. *See* also Rossbacher and Young, 520–25.

224. U.S.: Foreign Corrupt Practices Act of 1977, 15 U.S.C., Section 78dd-2(b). Routine governmental actions include obtaining permits, licenses, or other official documents; processing governmental papers, such as visa

and work orders; providing police protection, mail pick up, and delivery; loading and unloading cargo; and actions of a similar nature.

225. U.S.: Foreign Corrupt Practices Act of 1977, 15 U.S.C., Section 78dd-2(c).

226. U.S.: Foreign Corrupt Practices Act of 1977, 15 U.S.C., Section 78dd-2(e).

227. U.S.: Foreign Corrupt Practices Act of 1977, 15 U.S.C., Section 78dd-2(f).

228. Rossbacher and Young. Spring 1997. 15 Dick. J. Int'LL.509, 523–25.

229. Tanzania: Prevention of Corruption Act, Section 3(1).

230. Tanzania: Prevention of Corruption Act, Section 3(2).

231. Tanzania: Prevention of Corruption Act, Section 4.

232. Tanzania: Prevention of Corruption Act, Section 8(1).

233. Tanzania: Prevention of Corruption Act, Section 8(2).

234. Tanzania: Prevention of Corruption Act, Section 9(1).

235. Malawi: Corrupt Practices Act of 1995 (No. 18 of 1995), Section 28.

236. Malawi: Corrupt Practices Act of 1995 (No. 18 of 1995), Section 29.

237. Malawi: Corrupt Practices Act of 1995 (No. 18 of 1995), Section 30.

238. Malawi: Corrupt Practices Act of 1995 (No. 18 of 1995), Section 31.

239. Malawi: Corrupt Practices Act of 1995 (No. 18 of 1995), Section 32(1).

240. Malawi: Corrupt Practices Act of 1995 (No. 18 of 1995), Section 32(2).

241. Malawi: Corrupt Practices Act of 1995 (No. 18 of 1995), Section 53(1).

242. Hong Kong: Prevention of Bribery Act (Cap. 201).

243. Hong Kong: Prevention of Bribery Act, Section 4(1), (2).

244. Hong Kong: Prevention of Bribery Act, Section 2(1)(d).

245. Hong Kong: Prevention of Bribery Act, Section 24.

246. Hong Kong: Prevention of Bribery Act, Section 19.

247. Hong Kong: Prevention of Bribery Act, Section 4(1), (2).

248. Hong Kong: Prevention of Bribery Act, Section 5.

249. Hong Kong: Prevention of Bribery Act, Section 6.

250. Hong Kong: Prevention of Bribery Act, Section 7.

251. Hong Kong: Prevention of Bribery Act, Section 9.

252. Hong Kong: Prevention of Bribery Act, Section 10(1).

253. Hong Kong: Prevention of Bribery Act, Section 10(2).

254. Hong Kong: Prevention of Bribery Act, Section 10 12AA(1).

255. Hong Kong: Prevention of Bribery Act, Section 10 12AA(3).

256. Hong Kong: Prevention of Bribery Act, Section 12AA(4).

257. The Drug Trafficking Offenses Act of 1986 has been consolidated and reenacted in the Drug Trafficking Act of 1994. For a more detailed discussion of the money laundering provisions of this act, and of money-laundering offenses in general, *see* Rider, Barry A. K. 1995. "The Wages of Sin—Taking the Profit Out of Corruption—A British Perspective." *Dickinson Journal of International Law* 13:391—421.

258. U.K.: Criminal Justice Act of 1988, Section 93A(1), as amended by Criminal Justice Act of 1993, Section 29(1).

259. U.K.: Criminal Justice Act of 1988, Section 93A(4), as amended by Criminal Justice Act of 1993, Section 29(1).

260. U.K.: Criminal Justice Act of 1988, Section 93A(3), as amended by Criminal Justice Act of 1993, Section 29(1).

261. U.K.: Criminal Justice Act of 1988, Section 93C(1), as amended by Criminal Justice Act of 1993, Section 31.

262. U.K.: Criminal Justice Act of 1988, Section 93C(2), as amended by Criminal Justice Act of 1993, Section 31.

263. Du Pasquier, Shelby R. 1998. "The Swiss Anti-Money Laundering Legislation." *J. INT'L Banking L.* 13:160.

264. Swiss Criminal Code, Article 305 *bis*.

265. Du Pasquier 1998, 161.

266. Swiss Criminal Code, Article 305 *bis*, Paragraph 3.

267. Swiss Criminal Code, Article 305 *ter*, Paragraph 1.

268. Swiss Criminal Code, Article 305 *ter*, Paragraph 2.

269. Du Pasquier 1998, 162.

270. Switzerland: Money Laundering Act of 1997, Article 9(1). *See also* Du Pasquier 1998, 163.

271. Switzerland: Money Laundering Act of 1997, Article 9(2).

272. Switzerland: Money Laundering Act of 1997, Article 10(1).

273. Du Pasquier 1998, 164.

274. Switzerland: Money Laundering Act of 1997, Article 10(2).

275. Du Pasquier 1998, 163.

276. According to a recent report issued by the U.S. General Accounting Office (GAO), Citibank allegedly transferred as much as $100 million in drug money for the brother of the former Mexican president, Carlos Salinas de Gortari, without examining the source of funds or his financial background. According to the report, Citibank failed to follow its own procedures against

money laundering and facilitated a money managing system that disguised the origin, destination, and beneficial owner of the funds. It has been alleged that Citibank's failure to conduct the background check was a violation of its own internal KYC policy. Citibank has denied the charges. *See* 1998, December 4. "Citibank Called Lax on Salinas Money Trail." *The Washington Post*.

277. Latvia: Prevention of Proceeds Derived from Criminal Activity (December 18, 1997), Article 2.

278. Latvia: Prevention of Proceeds Derived from Criminal Activity (December 18, 1997), Article 28(1).

279. Latvia: Prevention of Proceeds Derived from Criminal Activity (December 18, 1997), Article 29.

280. Latvia: Prevention of Proceeds Derived from Criminal Activity (December 18, 1997), Article 37.

281. Latvia: Prevention of Proceeds Derived from Criminal Activity (December 18, 1997), Article 38.

282. Latvia: Prevention of Proceeds Derived from Criminal Activity (December 18, 1997), Article 4(10).

283. Latvia: Prevention of Proceeds Derived from Criminal Activity (December 18, 1997), Article 4.

284. Latvia: Prevention of Proceeds Derived from Criminal Activity (December 18, 1997), Article 17.

285. Latvia: Prevention of Proceeds Derived from Criminal Activity (December 18, 1997), Articles 6–10.

286. Latvia: Prevention of Proceeds Derived from Criminal Activity (December 18, 1997), Article 11.

287. Latvia: Prevention of Proceeds Derived from Criminal Activity (December 18, 1997), Articles 18, 19.

288. Hong Kong: Prevention of Bribery Act, Section10(1).

289. Tanzania: Prevention of Corruption Act, Section 9(1).

290. For a more detailed discussion of the rules governing reversal of the onus of proof and, in particular, their compatibility with human rights and related constitutional rights of accused parties, *see* de Speville 1997.

291. Hong Kong: Prevention of Bribery Act, Section 4(1), -(2).

292. Hong Kong: Prevention of Bribery Act, Section 24.

293. Malawi: Corrupt Practices Act of 1995, Section 45(2).

294. Tanzania: Prevention of Corruption Act, Section 10.

295. Malawi: Corrupt Practices Act of 1995, Section 32 (3).

296. Hong Kong: Prevention of Bribery Act, Section 10(2).

297. Malawi: Corrupt Practices Act of 1995, Section 34.

298. Tanzania: Prevention of Corruption Act, Sections 3, 4.

299. Hong Kong: Prevention of Bribery Act, Section 12.

300. Tanzania: Prevention of Corruption Act, Section 15.

301. Tanzania: Prevention of Corruption Act, Section 16.

302. Hong Kong: Prevention of Bribery Act, Section 14C.

303. Hong Kong: Prevention of Bribery Act, Section 12AA(1).

304. U.K.: Public Bodies Corrupt Practices Act of 1889, Section 7.

305. Tanzania: Prevention of Corruption Act, Section 2.

306. Malawi: Corrupt Practices Act of 1995, Section 3.

307. U.S: Bribery Law, 18 U.S.C., Section 201.

308. World Bank 1997.

309. World Bank 1997, Chapter 2.

310. Malawi: Corrupt Practices Act, *supra* note 200, sec.3.

311. U.S.: Foreign Corrupt Practices Act, Section 78dd-2(b).

312. Hong Kong: Prevention of Bribery Act, Section 19.

313. U.K. Law Commission. 1997, March 18. "Legislating the Criminal Code: Corruption." Law Commission Consultation Paper 145. Paragraph 8.52. London.

314. U.K. Law Commission 1997, March 18, Paragraph 8.29.

315. World Bank 1997, Chapter 2.

316. U.K. Law Commission 1997, March 18, Paragraphs 6.19–6.21.

317. U.K. Law Commission 1997, March 18, Chapter VII.

318. U.N. Document E/1978/115.

319. Economic and Social Council Resolution 1978/71, United Nations Economic and Social Council Official Records.

320. Economic and Social Council Resolution 1978/71, United Nations Economic and Social Council Official Records, Article 10.

321. U.N. 1996, December 16. "Declaration against Corruption and Bribery in International Commercial Transactions." 36 ILM 1043 (1997).

322. According to the U.N. declaration, bribery includes (a) the offer, promise, or giving of any payment, gift, or other advantage, directly or indirectly, by any private or public corporation, including a transnational corporation, or individual from a state to any public official or elected representative of another country as undue consideration for performing or refraining from the performance of that official's or representative's duties in connection with an international commercial transaction; and (b) the soliciting, demanding, accepting, or receiving, directly or indirectly, by any public official or elected representative of a state from any private or public corporation, including a transnational corporation, or individual from another country, of any payment, gift, or other advantage as undue consideration for performing or refraining from the performance of that official's or representative's duties in connection with an international commercial transaction.

323. Organization of American States (OAS). 1996, March 29. "Inter-American Convention against Corruption." 35 I.L.M. 724 (1996). Caracas.

324. OAS 1996, March 29, Article II.

325. OAS 1996, March 29, Article VI(1)(a)-(e).

326. OAS 1996, March 29, Article VIII.

327. OAS 1996, March 29, Article XI(a)–(d).

328. OAS 1996, March 29, Article III(4)–(6).

329. OAS 1996, March 29, Article III (1).

330. Organisation for Economic Co-operation and Development. 1997, May 23. "OECD Council Revised Recommendations C(97) 123/Final on Combating Bribery in International Business Transactions." 36 ILM 1016 (1997). Paris.

331 OECD Council Revised Recommendations 1997, May 23, Sections IV, V.

332 *See* OECD Council Revised Recommendations 1997, May 23, Annex to the Recommendation.

333. OECD Council Revised Recommendations 1997, May 23, Annex to the Recommendation, Element 1.

334. OECD Council Revised Recommendations 1997, May 23, Annex to the Recommendation, Element 4.

335. OECD Council Revised Recommendations 1997, May 23, Annex to the Recommendation, Element 5.

336. *See* Communiqué, G-7 meeting, Lyon, France.

337. Organisation for Economic Co-operation and Development. 1997, November 21. "Convention on Combating Bribery of Foreign Public Officials in International Business Transactions." 37 ILM 1 (1998). Paris.
This convention entered into force on February 15, 1999, in Bulgaria, Canada, Iceland, Germany, Greece, Hungary, Finland, Japan, Korea, Norway, the United Kingdom, and the United States.

338. Organisation for Economic Co-operation and Development 1997, November 21, Article 1.

339. Organisation for Economic Co-operation and Development 1997, November 21, Article 4.

340. Organisation for Economic Co-operation and Development 1997, November 21, Article 3.

341. Organisation for Economic Co-operation and Development 1997, November 21, Article 7.

342. Organisation for Economic Co-operation and Development 1997, November 21, Article 12.

343. The OECD Ministerial Council had agreed to take collective action to confront the problem of bribery in May 1994 and, more particularly, had adopted a recommendation against tax deductibility for bribes to foreign government officials. In recommending this action, the OECD Council of Ministers, recognized at the time that, although most of its member countries have legislation that makes the bribing of their public officials and the taking of bribes by these officials criminal offenses, only a few had laws making the bribing of foreign officials a punishable offense, as it is in the United States. They established a Working Group on Bribery in International Business Transactions to examine, among other things, specific issues relating to bribery and carry out regular reviews of actions taken by member countries in the implementation of the antibribery recommendation for bribes to foreign government officials.

344. *See* Council of Europe. 1998, December 1. "Explanatory Report on the Criminal Law Convention." MGC(98)40. Strasbourg.

345. Council of Europe. 1998, December 1. "Explanatory Report on the Criminal Law Convention." MGC(98)40. Strasbourg.

346. *See* Global Coalition for Africa. 1997, November 2. "Corruption and Development in Africa." Document GCA/PF/No. 2/11/1997. Maputo, Mozambique.
The paper refers also to the mechanisms for dealing with corruption in Botswana, which is hailed as a country with a comparatively low level of corruption. Botswana has an independent entity to combat corruption, which has been highly effective in dealing with corruption cases. *See* Global Coalition for Africa. 1997, November 2, Annex 1.

347. Global Coalition for Africa. 1997, November 2, Annex 1.

348. Global Coalition for Africa. 1997, November 2, Co-Chairperson's Closing Statement at 5, Document GCA/11/1997.

349. Global Coalition for Africa. 1997, November 2, "Co-chairperson's Closing Statement," 5–6.

350. GCA. 1999, February 23. "Report of the Meeting on Collaborative Frameworks to Address Corruption." Washington, D.C..

351. The Lima Declaration against Corruption (September 11, 1997), Declaration of the 8th International Conference against Corruption held in Lima, Peru from 7–11, 1997. (Lima Declaration.) (http://www.transparency.de/lacc/e-limadecl.html)

352. Lima Declaration, 1997 October, 3–7, Paragraphs 1—20.

353. Lima Declaration, 1997 October, Declaration 6.1.

354. Lima Declaration, 1997 October, Declaration 6.2.

355. Lima Declaration, 1997 October, Declaration 6.3.

356. Lima Declaration, 1997 October, Declaration 6.7.

357. Lima Declaration, 1997 October, 10–13.

358. *See, generally,* Lima Declaration, 1997 October, 31–40.

359. The Shawcross Commission Report, which was presented and adopted at the 131st session of the Council of the ICC (November 29, 1977), became the Rules of Conduct.

360. *See* International Chamber of Commerce. 1996, May. "Extortion and Bribery in International Business Transactions." Report adopted on March 26, 1996 by the Executive Board at its 83rd session.

361. *See* Shihata 1996, 25.

www.ingramcontent.com/pod-product-compliance
Lightning Source LLC
Chambersburg PA
CBHW020708270326
41928CB00005B/322